Promoting Integrated and Transformative Assessment

Promoting Integrated and Transformative Assessment

A *Deeper Focus on Student Learning*

Catherine M. Wehlburg

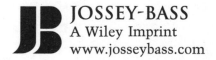

JOSSEY-BASS
A Wiley Imprint
www.josseybass.com

Published by Jossey-Bass
A Wiley Imprint
989 Market Street, San Francisco, CA 94103-1741—www.josseybass.com

Readers should be aware that Internet Web sites offered as citations and/or sources for further information may have changed or disappeared between the time this was written and when it is read.

Limit of Liability/Disclaimer of Warranty: While the publisher and author have used their best efforts in preparing this book, they make no representations or warranties with respect to the accuracy or completeness of the contents of this book and specifically disclaim any implied warranties of merchantability or fitness for a particular purpose. No warranty may be created or extended by sales representatives or written sales materials. The advice and strategies contained herein may not be suitable for your situation. You should consult with a professional where appropriate. Neither the publisher nor author shall be liable for any loss of profit or any other commercial damages, including but not limited to special, incidental, consequential, or other damages.

Jossey-Bass books and products are available through most bookstores. To contact Jossey-Bass directly call our Customer Care Department within the U.S. at 800-956-7739, outside the U.S. at 317-572-3986, or fax 317-572-4002.

Jossey-Bass also publishes its books in a variety of electronic formats. Some content that appears in print may not be available in electronic books.

Library of Congress Cataloging-in-Publication Data

Wehlburg, Catherine.
    Promoting integrated and transformative assessment : a deeper focus on student learning / Catherine M. Wehlburg.
        p.   cm.
    Includes bibliographical references and index.
    ISBN 978-0-470-26135-4 (cloth)
        1. Education, Higher—United States—Evaluation.   2. Educational evaluation—United States.   3. Learning—Evaluation.   4. Educational accountability—United States.   I. Title.
    LB2822.75.W445   2008
    378.1'66—dc22

                                                                    2008010931

Printed in the United States of America
FIRST EDITION
HB Printing   10 9 8 7 6 5 4 3 2 1

The Jossey-Bass
Higher and Adult Education Series

Contents

To my husband, George Krasowsky;
my daughter, Brooke; and
my colleagues at Texas Christian University

Preface

In the academic year 1998–1999, I was fortunate enough to be able to take a sabbatical from Stephens College (Columbia, Missouri) and join the staff at the American Association for Higher Education (AAHE). Shortly after arriving, I was asked to take on the responsibility of planning the 1999 AAHE Assessment Conference. Of course, I responded that I would love to do that. After all, how hard could that be? During the months of preparation for the conference, however, I realized that it was very difficult, but that it was worth every bit of time and energy that it took.

During my year with AAHE, I was able to have regular meetings with Ted Marchese, who introduced me to several philosophers and many others whose work has been important to how higher education thinks about teaching and learning. As part of the preparatory process for the conference, I spoke with many people from across the United States and beyond our borders. Their thoughts, ideas, and constructs about education in general were almost an ongoing postgraduate seminar for me, and I thought about how we are assessing student learning and why we are doing it with the methods that we currently use.

During this time, I was also interested in the pedagogy side of the educational process. I worked with others in the field of faculty development, and I realized how many of us separate the teaching part of the process from the assessing of learning part. But good teaching requires knowing what students are learning, and to know what students are learning requires assessing them in some way. Our master teachers already do this, and it shows in the modifications that they make to their courses. But the assessment process has almost always been imposed on institutions by outside forces, and so faculty who were already assessing student learning on a regular and ongoing basis seemed to balk at the idea of assessing at the program or institutional level for an accreditation visit or a self-study.

Why would this be? Assessment and teaching/learning are two sides of the same coin. Why gather information for assessment purposes if you are not going to use those data to improve a course or a program? At the same time, if faculty already are gathering student learning information in their courses, why can't those data be used to look across a program at student learning? As I read the literature and talked with more people, it became clear that work in transformative assessment was already happening. But it often was not called "assessment" or viewed as such.

As the executive director of the Office for Assessment and Quality Enhancement at Texas Christian University, I work with faculty daily and have seen how they work with students to engage them in disciplinary thinking and content. Similarly I have watched those in student affairs provide numerous learning opportunities for students in leadership, understanding diversity, and becoming responsible citizens. So much of this is happening across many institutions, but we often do not include nonacademic assessment data when looking at the overall institutional effectiveness in ways that will promote quality enhancement. As a periodic evaluator for the Commission on Colleges of the Southern Association of Colleges and Schools and a past consultant-evaluator for the Higher Learning Commission of the North Central Association, I have seen many institutions that are gathering information to look good rather than gathering information to grow.

We cannot continue to use assessment data to prove to others how wonderful our own institutions are. We must be gathering information that will give us direction in terms of what areas need attention. If higher education is going to meet the changing needs of society, we must keep looking at what we are doing, how well we are doing it, and where we need to be.

Since about the mid-1980s when regional (and other) accrediting bodies started requiring assessment plans and results, most institutions have developed assessment plans, hired assessment personnel, and gathered a lot of data. What often happens, however, is that these assessment plans are added on top of the other teaching/learning/service/research activities on campus, so assessment is often not embedded into the framework of the institution and not used by the institution in any ongoing way.

Typically, then, faculty, staff, and entire institutions work diligently in the time leading up to an accreditation visit to gather and analyze information, create end-of-year reports, and go into overdrive to prepare for any upcoming visit for reaccreditation. What is missing from this frenzy is an integrated and ongoing system for gathering meaningful and appropriate assessment information that will help to guide the decisions that the institution makes about student learning.

Enhancing student learning should be the priority, with documenting evidence for accreditation a secondary purpose. The process for assessment planning should be done for the institution's benefit first and foremost. In order for this type of system to work, it must be embedded and integrated into the regular cycle of institutional events, course revisions, and student life, and it must lead to meaningful and transformational aspects of learning and of the campus community.

Chapter One defines *transformative assessment* as an appropriate, meaningful, sustainable, flexible, and ongoing process that will inform decision making and use data for improvement, with the potential for substantive change. This chapter places assessment within the current context of higher education, with all of the external forces asking for accountability and the internal forces that focus on the individual and unique mission and purpose of the institution.

Chapter Two discusses several of the historical reasons that assessment has been through as many revisions as it has. This chapter gives an overview of several of the precursors to the assessment movement and the challenges to integrating assessment into the campus culture. In addition, it explores different (and sometimes conflicting) definitions of *assessment* and *effectiveness*.

Chapter Three begins with a discussion of the many roles that faculty are asked to fill and some of the typical concerns that often surface as assessment is incorporated into an institutional structure. The organizational structure of any institution is an important factor if assessment is going to move from a top-down mandated requirement to one that is focused on measuring student learning in order to improve it.

Chapter Four contends that it is crucial to have faculty support and faculty leadership for transformative assessment to be successful. It provides some ideas and examples for creating an atmosphere that will foster faculty collaboration and leadership in departmental and institutional assessment processes.

Chapter Five explores integrating an assessment process across the entire campus. Suggestions for effective collaboration among faculty, administration, and student affairs staff are given, along with specific examples of successful work across campuses. Collaboration can be beneficial to the institution, those working with faculty and student affairs, and the students who will benefit from any results of transformative assessment.

An effectiveness plan should provide the institution with enough information to make good decisions. When this plan is based on assessment data, the resulting decisions are likely to be successful because they will be grounded in the facts and other information available. Chapter Six looks at methods to create an institutional effectiveness plan that is closely aligned with the overall mission and individual needs of the institution.

Chapter Seven provides models of implementation for transformative assessment. In addition, this chapter shares some lessons learned from the process that may help to guide institutions that are moving toward transformative assessment.

The process used to embed assessment activities within existing structures is the topic of Chapter Eight. Being able to assess overall student learning outcomes while also providing information to faculty about individual student learning and giving students feedback about their own performance is possible. This chapter discusses the importance of using authentic assessment tools as a method to better inform decision making.

Chapter Nine offers a view of the potential synergy that can occur between assessment for accountability and assessment for transformation. It also discusses the role of regional accreditation in the national conversation about institutional effectiveness and how individual institutions are by definition a part of the process.

The book ends in Chapter Ten with an overview of the issues that will confront higher education and the assessment of institutional effectiveness as we move forward. Among them are student matriculation patterns, technology, increasing needs for accountability, and the understanding that learning is a complex process that cannot be effectively measured by a multiple-choice style.

Although the chapters are designed to be read sequentially, readers are invited to read the book in any order. Transformative assessment can be a messy and time-consuming process, and when it is successful, it is rarely done in a straight line. Reading about transformative assessment should be similarly flexible.

Acknowledgments

Several people have worked with me over the past several years and have given me wonderful ideas, support, and collegial conversations about the use of transformative assessment. First, I thank Mary Kitterman, vice president for academic affairs at Cottey College. Mary was the first to broach the concept of working with the Stephens College self-study and reaccreditation process. Robert Badel, president at Jamestown College, also gave me opportunities to explore the connections between assessment and the teaching/learning process. I thank Theodore Marchese as well. Ted was the vice president at the American Association for Higher Education when I spent a one-year sabbatical there. His thoughtful guidance was instrumental in fostering a desire to see the assessment process as much more than an accreditation requirement. I also thank Jim Anker, who supported the concept of this book before a single word was written.

I especially thank Zoanne Hogg at Texas Christian University, who read, edited, and commented on every word from every draft of every chapter. I am very grateful for her ongoing support, friendship, and wonderful editing skills. Likewise, Billie Hara has given me ongoing support and encouragement in all of my writing. Our Friday afternoon meetings have been instrumental in completing this book. Edward McNertney, director of the core curriculum at Texas Christian University, has been a wonderful colleague whose support and interest in transformative assessment have been meaningful to me.

Finally, I thank my family. My husband, George, and daughter, Brooke, were patient and loving with me even when I had to bring a laptop to several weekend events. At the time of this writing, Brooke is seven years old, and she thinks that everyone must lug around a laptop constantly "just in case." As she was playing make-believe with her friends, she was using one of her bags as a briefcase, and she pulled out a cardboard box top and said that it was her keyboard and that she needed to "make a few notes."

About the Author

Catherine M. Wehlburg is executive director of the Office for Assessment and Quality Enhancement at Texas Christian University. She taught psychology and educational psychology courses for more than a decade, serving as department chair for some of that time, and then branched into faculty development and assessment after serving as the self-study coordinator for her initial institution. In addition, she has worked with both the Higher Learning Commission of the North Central Association and the Commission on Colleges of the Southern Association of Colleges and Schools as an outside evaluator. She has served as editor of *To Improve the Academy*, and she regularly presents workshops on assessment, transformation, and teaching and learning. She earned her Ph.D. in educational psychology from the University of Florida.

Promoting Integrated and Transformative Assessment

What Is Transformative Assessment?

The term *assessment* does not bring happiness and joy to most people in higher education. Assessment has, for decades, been a required method for gathering information to show accountability to certain stakeholders, most notably, the accreditation process. It is a time-consuming process that has often been viewed as a waste of time. "Wait until this passes, and we can go back to doing things the way we want to!" is something that more than one faculty member, college president, and board member has said. If students are asked to think about "institutional assessment," they rarely have any ideas about it. Yet hundreds of conferences have been held and thousands of books and articles written on this topic. How can something be so disliked by faculty and college administrators and ignored by students, yet be hugely popular in terms of conferences and publications? More important, what has assessment done for higher education? Is higher education better because of all of the time and money spent on assessment-related issues? Has this time been well spent and meaningful? Unfortunately the answer to these questions in most situations is no.

Higher education has not used assessment information well. Yes, data have been collected and filed. Accrediting visitors have searched through hundreds of thousands of binders, files, Web sites, and folders. Countless hours of faculty and administrative time have been spent on collecting data for accountability purposes. Thousands of students have taken pretests, posttests, and satisfaction surveys and attended focus groups designed to discover what they are (and are not) liking, learning, and remembering.

But very little of this has made a difference in student learning. The teaching and learning process has not changed much. Yes, technology plays a greater role than it did a decade ago, but this is not the result of using assessment data. As a matter of fact, there is much that is still unknown about the impact of using technology for teaching on the learning that actually occurs. It seems that higher education has been assessing for many of the wrong reasons. "It may well be that undergraduate education has not suffered any discernible decline in quality over the past 50 or 100 years. But is that really a satisfactory outcome? Most human enterprise improves with time and experience. . . . Given the vastly expanded resources colleges have acquired, thanks to growing private donations, steadily rising tuition, and massive infusions of federal financial aid, isn't it fair to expect the quality of education to improve as well?" (Bok, 2006, p. 29).

Data have been collected (and filed, piled, and stored) for the benefit of others. But it seems clear that higher education has not done a very good job of using assessment data to improve student learning or the quality of the undergraduate experience.

Lee Shulman (2007) indicated that assessment and its use for accountability is actually a way to tell the story of the department or unit for which the assessment is done. In Shulman's metaphor of storytelling, assessment becomes a means for building the narrative that can be shared outside the department: "The story told by an assessment is thus ultimately a function of the dimensions of measurement that determine the possible directions the narrative might take. So accountability requires that we take responsibility for the story we commit ourselves to telling. We must make public the rationale for choosing that story as opposed to alternative narratives. . . . Only then should we defend the adequacy of the forms of measurement and documentation we employ to warrant the narratives we offer" (p. 22). Viewing the assessment process as a means to sharing information is essential. Nevertheless, the assessment process should not be developed only for others.

Assessment must provide meaningful and appropriate information to those who created the process.

Why Hasn't Assessment Been More Successful?

Tom Angelo (1999) proposes several reasons that the assessment movement has not created the type of enhanced student learning that many thought that it would: "I'll argue that most assessment efforts have resulted in little learning improvement because they have been implemented without a clear vision of what 'higher' or 'deeper' learning is and without an understanding of how assessment can promote such learning" (p. 3). In addition, assessment is often seen as a mechanistic process, one that treats learning as an assembly-line process rather than an attempt to measure something extremely complex. Higher education, in an attempt to provide an easy-to-use measurement of learning, has often oversimplified the process. This oversimplification has led to a certain amount of disgust. "No matter how much they [outcomes assessment practices] purport to be about 'standards' or student 'needs,' they are in fact scams run by bloodless bureaucrats who, steeped in jargon like 'mapping learning goals' and 'closing the loop,' do not understand the holistic nature of a good college education" (Fendrich, 2007, p. B6). It is truly unfortunate that some view assessment as only a bureaucratic process rather than something that could be created to inform our discussions about teaching and learning. However, as Shulman reminds us, "We are limited in our recountings by the instruments we use to count" (2007, p. 22). The process for assessment can be seen as only about accountability for others, as Fendrich suggests. But assessment can also be about transformation, about the journey toward our vision of what higher education should be.

Another reason the assessment process may not have produced more successful programs is that some people, "probably conditioned by program evaluation and accreditation experiences, see assessment as a necessary, periodic bother, like a visit to the accountant at tax time" (Angelo, 1999, p. 4). The thought that the assessment process is insinuated into the regular academic structure has caused some to view the process as "a judgmental tool for punishment [rather than a] source of illumination" (Musil, 1992, p. 4).

Without appropriate and sustainable measures that can give useful information to those who need it, assessment can become something that measures only the easily counted and not the conceptual level of information that is the most meaningful. Is it any wonder that not all within the higher education community have embraced assessment?

Closing the Feedback Loop

One way to ensure that the assessment process gives information to those who create it is to make certain that the data resulting from the process are used to make informed decisions about the department or unit. There have been calls to "close the assessment loop" for decades. But why isn't this being done on a regular basis? Why don't all college and university campuses have this in place? The answers to these deceptively simple questions are, not surprisingly, complex. These answers stem from the different purposes of assessment: using assessment for accountability for an external audience and assessing student learning on a local level to contribute to learning.

Assessment at the local level has always occurred. Faculty often modify a particular part of a course they are teaching or an individual class period based on student confusion or comprehension. This type of assessment is often not even recognized as assessment of student learning by many faculty; it is just part of the process of teaching. In this assessment-for-learning paradigm, there is no dishonor in finding out that students are not understanding any given material. When this happens, good teachers make modifications: they review material in class or add reading assignments, for example.

However, knowing about student learning at the local level (assessment for learning) may not ever enter into what becomes used as assessment for accountability. Instead the assessment-for-accountability data that are shared are often used to show the general public, stakeholders, and accreditors that institutions are doing a good job: in other words, that students are learning what the institution or department says that they should be learning. As a result, assessment for accountability does not often ask the hard questions or try to measure concepts that are difficult to quantify. These two purposes of assessment are often at odds with each other, which makes it difficult to close the feedback loop.

The phrase "closing the feedback loop" of an assessment cycle refers to the process of using results from appropriate and meaningful student learning outcomes to make modifications in the teaching and learning activities within a course. These should lead to changes in the results of the student learning outcomes in the next cycle (see Figure 1.1). Unfortunately, institutions and faculty often stop short of completely closing the loop. They create outcomes, they measure those outcomes, and they may even analyze these outcomes. But then these results are written up in a report and filed away in a dusty drawer or stored on a computer, never to be seen again.

This process amounts to a lot of work with very little impact. But why would anyone go to the trouble of developing, measuring, and analyzing outcomes, and then not use that information to make curricular or pedagogical changes? Here, the answers are bureaucratically straightforward.

Although the concept of closing the feedback loop has been discussed for quite some time, a new concept of the assessment spiral has been used to describe the process where "at the close of each feedback loop, quality will have increased and moved the spiral up to the next level" (Wehlburg, 2007, p. 1).

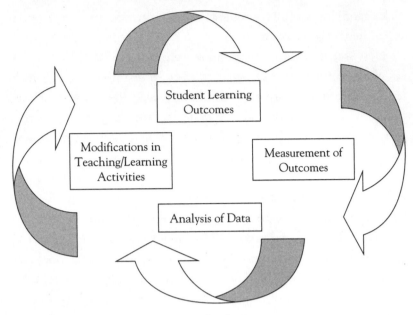

Student Learning
Outcomes

Modifications in
Teaching/Learning
Activities

Measurement of
Outcomes

Analysis of Data

Figure 1.1   The Assessment Feedback Loop

Accreditation as a Top-Down Process

Accreditation movements began in the late nineteenth century and focused on minimal standards (Alstete, 2004). Following this, accreditation organizations often focused on a quantitative approach (seen as more "objective" than a qualitative approach) to measuring elements of a campus that would provide calculable "input" variables (for example, graduation rates, numbers of books in the library, amount of an institution's endowment). A great deal of attention was paid to the use of assessment data for accountability. Institutions essentially were being asked to show that they were doing what they said they were doing. But in the 1980s, more attention was being paid to the things that were not necessarily easily countable, and accreditation organizations and higher education in general began to move toward the qualitative areas that are such a large part of postsecondary education.

As part of this shift, more attention was being paid to student learning. Accreditation organizations began to require institutions to have an assessment plan that outlined what students should learn as a result of a particular program of study. And since these organizations were requiring assessment plans and assessment reports, these became highly important to higher education administrators, which meant that assessment plans and measures of student learning became important. Accountability was still a driving force behind the purposes of this type of assessment. However, missing in many of these early approaches to the assessment of student learning was requiring the data to be used in making changes in pedagogy or curriculum.

As a result, assessment offices sprouted up all over the country, and much emphasis was placed on creating and measuring student learning outcomes. Unfortunately, the purpose of assessment on many campuses was to demonstrate compliance with a regional accreditor. And once the outcomes were created, measured, and written in reports, the job was considered done. In the mid-1990s, visiting teams of accreditation evaluators would come to a campus, look for assessment plans and the resulting data, and hear much rhetoric about assessment. However, in many cases, the team members found that there was no real culture of using assessment data to benefit student learning. Cecelia Lopez, formerly the associate director of the Higher Learning Commission, North Central Association of Colleges and Schools, analyzed reports from many visiting teams and used these results to create an assessment culture matrix (Higher Learning Commission/NCA, 2003). This matrix allows institutions to determine where they are in the development of an institutional culture that uses assessment results for making meaningful changes that may enhance student learning. According to Lopez (2002), "The matrix depicts three Levels of Implementation of assessment programs, each with four associated Patterns of Characteristics" (p. 358). Characteristics of institutions at the first level (Beginning Implementation) show no "institution-wide understanding of the strategies to be used in conducting an effective assessment program." In addition, "quantitative and qualitative measures are not aligned with academic program goals and objectives" (para. 1).

As assessment practices have become more institutionalized, the rhetoric of more advanced levels of implementation of assessment has become more common, but actual practice at many institutions following a successful reaccreditation visit has not demonstrated a true embracing of a culture of assessment. Instead, faculty may say things like, "Whew, I'm glad that whole assessment thing is over! Now I can get back to my real work of teaching and research." This type of sentiment unfortunately leads to a filing away of assessment reports and checking them off as completed rather than finding a way to use the information to enhance teaching and learning.

Assessment of student learning outcomes can show how much or how well a student is learning, but it does not focus on the "input" part of the teaching/learning equation. Assessment data do not usually indicate what teaching methods are working, whether class size had an impact on student learning, or how much time a student spent in preparation and studying. The results of assessment give only part of the picture of student learning.

Teaching Enhancement as a Bottom-Up Process

Teaching enhancement (sometimes called faculty development) has always played an important part in the teaching/learning process, but not until the 1970s did specific programs designed to improve teaching began to grow into specific professional development programs with institutional support (Gaff, 1975; Centra, 1976; Bergquist & Phillips, 1975). Now, many institutions have teaching centers and associated programs that are designed to increase teaching effectiveness and student learning.

Many faculty participate in workshops and programs that are designed to improve their teaching and help them actively engage students in the course content. In addition, most academic disciplines have teaching-focused journals in addition to ones that are research or practice based. The growth of faculty development over the last thirty years has been astounding. Many books have been written on group discussion, student engagement, and incorporating active learning into a course. These types of practices are excellent methods to help faculty modify their teaching and better engage students.

At many institutions, faculty participation in teaching enhancement activities is not mandated. Faculty can choose to attend a workshop, schedule a time with a teaching consultant, or have their class observed and get feedback. With the possible exception of required new faculty orientations, many of the participants in faculty development activities do so because they want to. They choose to modify or enhance their teaching. Sometimes they do it to make a change in their course because of something new a colleague is doing, or they have received poor course evaluation results and want to improve their scores. Some faculty are looking for ways to increase student learning in their course or want to engage their students better. For these faculty, teaching enhancement activities can increase their satisfaction with their courses and their teaching, and this can certainly improve student learning.

But because it is usually not a mandatory practice, faculty who might most need developing often choose not to participate. An informal look at many teaching centers shows that a majority of faculty do not actively participate in faculty development programs on a regular basis. So although faculty development activities seem to have a positive impact on teaching behaviors (and potentially student engagement and learning), many faculty do not take part in the process.

For those who do participate in teaching centers or other faculty development activities, there is a lack of empirical evidence about how this contributes to student learning. Following many development workshops or events, faculty are asked to complete an evaluation of the workshop. These satisfaction ratings are helpful in designing the next event or workshop, but they provide no evidence of change in the faculty member's teaching. And even if the faculty member makes a change in teaching or learning activities, what impact does that have on student learning? So we know that faculty development activities have an impact on teaching (at best), but it is very difficult to determine what impact that has on student learning. Faculty development activities are certainly related to student learning, but they are only indirectly measured. This is another part of the student learning equation. For example, faculty who are working to modify their courses to enhance student learning do not usually look at results from alumni surveys or other areas that would potentially have longer-term learning outcomes (Wehlburg, 2006). And it is possible that information about what alumni indicate was important learning could benefit the course modification process.

Meeting in the Middle: Using Assessment to Inform Teaching and Learning

It seems, then, that the assessment of student learning process has become important to institutions but that the information is not always used to enhance student learning. Although calls to close the feedback loop have been going on for some time, many institutions still have little interaction between those who collect and report assessment data and those who focus on improving teaching and learning. It is essential, however, for assessment data to inform teaching/learning decisions and for faculty to create student learning outcomes with a focus on what is important for students to learn. Without this interaction, a lot of effort is going to be spent on collecting data with little impact on teaching and learning.

Assessment is important, and the accreditation associations are mandating that institutions have a process and use it. Therefore, most postsecondary institutions are regularly, perhaps grudgingly, collecting information on student learning. But this information should be collected anyway, and many faculty have been doing this all along. The information that they have collected on student learning, however, has been used to measure an individual student's performance in class rather than looking at multiple students across time to see how well they are doing in general with regard to departmental student learning outcomes. There is an opportunity to use existing student work products to evaluate the student for a grade in the class and aggregate those data by looking across students to see what they are learning as a group. By integrating assessment with teaching activities, assessment data can be used for what this information was originally intended: to know how well students are doing and to use that knowledge to make changes in curriculum, pedagogy, or course design.

By meeting in the middle, where student learning outcomes are measured by using student work artifacts already embedded in courses, departments and institutions can develop outcomes that reflect what is actually happening without adding much testing time. One thing that is clear, however, is that "assessment techniques are of little use unless and until local academic cultures value self-examination, reflection, and continuous improvement" (Angelo, 1999, p. 5).

Assessment and *accreditation* are terms that often are used interchangeably, but they are very different. Accreditation is "a process by which an institution of postsecondary education evaluates its educational activities, in whole or in part, and seeks an independent judgment to confirm that it substantially achieves its objectives and is generally equal in quality to comparable institutions or specialized units" (Young, Chambers, & Kells, 1983, p. 21). The accreditation process uses assessment data, but it also uses other levels of information that focus on issues other than student learning. A look at any of the regional accrediting bodies will show that library resources, instructional technologies, and faculty credentials, for example, are crucial to the accreditation process.

Although these may be indirectly measured by assessment, the accreditation process is important because institutions must demonstrate that they have the resources necessary to fulfill their mission. Assessment is a necessary but not sufficient part of the accreditation process.

Transformative Assessment

Student learning assessment is "the systematic collection of information about student learning, using the time, knowledge, expertise, and resources available, in order to inform decisions about how to improve learning" (Walvoord, 2004, p. 2). The key in this definition is that assessment is done for the purpose of informing decisions about improving student learning. Assessment data have often been used for accountability to others, but their explicit and primary purpose is to inform decisions about student learning. Higher education, and education in K–12 schools, has allowed this alternative and secondary use of assessment data. And that secondary purpose has become, in many cases, the perceived primary purpose of assessment. On many campuses, assessment is now seen as something imposed on the institution by the administration and by others (those in the regional and specialized accreditation process). Assessment of student learning has become something that is done for others rather than for its original purpose. "But with the publication in September 2006 of the report of the Commission on the Future of Higher Education, suddenly the use of assessment of individual students to improve learning on a single campus is not enough. We must also provide evidence of student learning that can be compared across campuses" (Banta, 2007a, p. 3).

It is time to change this situation. Assessment data can and will be used for accountability. Parents, potential students, and the public deserve to know what higher education is doing. Accountability has an important role. But to gather assessment data only to show others what is occurring seems to be a hugely time-consuming task that will never intentionally inform decision making about the teaching and learning process. Assessment that is designed to provide information to transform teaching and learning is both necessary and essential.

Transformative assessment is a process that will inform decision making that is appropriate, meaningful, sustainable, flexible and ongoing and will use data for improvement with the potential for substantive change. Although the data that are collected can also be used to demonstrate outcomes to others, transformative assessment is principally focused on how to enhance student learning. In order to be effective, each element of transformative assessment is essential, but because of the differing missions, institutional cultures, and needs, each may be implemented differently.

Transformative Assessment Must Be Appropriate

The word *appropriate* is defined by the *American Heritage Dictionary* (2002) as "suitable for a particular person, condition, occasion, or place." What this means to the assessment process is that specific outcomes for a course, department, or institution will differ from other outcomes written for different purposes. An institution's mission is a unique statement of purpose. The institutional-level outcomes must reflect that institutional identity, and the outcomes that are measured should align with the mission statement.

Cookie-cutter approaches to assessment will almost always fail to become transformative processes because the outcomes used will not be appropriate to the institution or department that is using them. Department-level outcomes will be specific to the content and context of that department at that specific institution. A biology department's outcomes from a small, private, liberal arts college may be similar to a biology department from a large, research university with a large graduate student population, but they will probably not be identical. The context of the institutional mission will have an impact on the department mission statement and resulting outcomes. The same holds true for outcomes for specific courses within a department.

Knowing that the assessment process is appropriate and focused on the unique perspectives of different institutions will help to ensure that the process is used to inform the decision making regarding teaching and learning.

Transformative Assessment Must Be Meaningful

Without a meaningful approach to assessment, the process is almost always doomed to becoming an add-on task done for bureaucratic purposes. Meaningful assessment practices will result in data that will be used because the decision makers care about the results. If an institution has a focus on leadership, outcomes would likely be developed that would indicate levels and types of leadership that students would develop. Following this, measures of how many students are leaders might be an important data point. An institution that values leadership will likely care about the results of this measure.

Many doctoral students who are gathering data for their largest research project ever await the first results with bated breath. Getting those survey responses or seeing the lab results is quite exciting—and it is exciting because the event is meaningful. Assessment results could be viewed in the same way if they are truly meaningful. Institution and department assessment plans and assessment measures should result in data that faculty and staff care about. Knowing the percentage of students accepted for graduate school or seeing test results from graduating seniors should provide information useful for making curricular and planning decisions. If the data collected end up being stored, then they are not meaningful, and going to the effort of collecting them probably is a waste of time, resources, and space. But developing outcomes and measures that are important will help focus on what needs to be changed or enhanced. These are the types of data that will cause transformation to take place.

Transformative Assessment Must Be Sustainable

No matter how meaningful and appropriate an assessment plan is, it will not be used for longer than one cycle if it cannot be sustained. Often as an institution gets ready for an accreditation visit, elaborate and time-consuming assessment structures are put into place. Although the data that are collected may be useful and important, if the added time and resources to do the assessment are too great, the assessment process will not be sustained after a successful reaccreditation. And once again assessment will be seen as something that is done only for the purposes of gaining a particular accreditation status rather than as an ongoing, embedded process for benefiting teaching and learning.

Making an assessment process sustainable means that it has to fit into the regular cycle of the institution. Beginning a program just prior to an accreditation visit will likely result in an assessment process focused on accountability rather than transformation. The assessment planning and data collection must be something that can be done regularly. They must become institutionalized and embedded.

Institutions typically have a huge amount of data about student learning at any given time. Some of the information has been gathered by third-party vendors (for example, National Survey of Student Engagement or Cooperative Institutional Research Program data), but much of it is already embedded in the regular cycle of the university. Student papers and exams, alumni surveys, and participation rates are some examples of data that probably are already being collected. By using data in multiple ways, the assessment plan can become more sustainable. Every academic department requires students to submit work for courses. Homework problems, papers, exams, presentations, and even in-class discussions can demonstrate what a student knows in a relatively authentic way. These examples of student work are usually used for determining an individual student's grade, but they can also be lifted out of the course setting and used to evaluate student learning outcomes across a department or even an institution. If those data are already being collected, a huge hurdle can be overcome when developing an assessment plan. Similarly, by sampling student work to measure a particular outcome, a faculty assessment committee can spend less time reading papers (for example) as part of the assessment plan while still gathering enough evidence of student learning to share with the entire department. The assessment planning process becomes more sustainable because it is something that can be viewed as requiring a reasonable amount of time to spend on the project.

Transformative Assessment Must Be Flexible and Ongoing

Once an assessment plan is developed, measures measured, and findings used, what happens? If the assessment process is flexible, the assessment results should suggest modifications for the next cycle. It should be a formative process that is reevaluated at the beginning and the end of each cycle. This flexibility of the assessment plan will lead to its sustainability, which will promote the ongoing (or neverending) characteristic of a transformative assessment program.

Just as any course taught might be modified each semester based on course evaluations, student responses on exams, and needs of the department, so should departmental and institutional assessment plans be modified. If a department is working on enhancing student learning, that learning will probably increase in particular areas. This should prompt the faculty to raise the bar in terms of student learning outcomes. What once might have been acceptable may no longer be the appropriate level of student learning. If assessment is working to transform higher education, there should be a corresponding increase (quantitatively or qualitatively) in what and how much students are learning and how they are using the information they have gained during college. Transformative assessment should be flexible and ongoing enough to demonstrate the assessment spiral: "Many campuses with active assessment programs have moved away from the two dimensions of the feedback circle and are thinking of assessment as an upward spiral, still identifying goals and outcomes, still measuring those outcomes, but with ever-increasing improvement of the quality of student learning as the spiral moves upward" (Wehlburg, 2007, p. 1). A quality assessment plan that provides information to a department or institution will result in an upward spiral of ever-increasing student quality. This will require flexibility in the process of assessment planning (and replanning) and an understanding that the assessment plan is part of an ongoing process and is not cast in stone.

Transformative Assessment Must Be Used for Improvement with the Potential for Substantive Change

Clearly if an assessment program is going to be successful, the data must be used for improvement, and there must be potential for change. Assessment is not a product or an end; it is a process that leads to enhanced teaching and learning, and informed decision making focused on the mission and values of a specific institution. The data that come from the assessment process are not meaningful unless they can be used to determine what a particular department or institution can do to increase the quality (and perhaps quantity) of student learning. "Doing assessment" is very different from using the results of an assessment process. If faculty and administrators think of assessment as something that must be done for an outside body (accreditation or a board of trustees, for example), the assessment process will never be truly transformative. But when the ongoing assessment planning provides information about what needs improvement, transformation that is based on student learning data can be accomplished.

Transformative assessment can provide evidence of areas that are not being accomplished at the levels that the institution or department wants. In the past, this might have been seen as a failure because students did not learn what was expected. But since when did it become a bad thing to fail at something? When children learn to walk, they fall many times before they are successful, but they keep trying until they get it. Students too fail at many things before they succeed. If students knew everything before they came to college, there would not be much for them to do academically once they got into their institution. But the truth is that students do not know all that they need to know. This means that they have to learn it, and in learning it, they have to practice it correctly. First (and second and third) drafts of papers are needed as students learn writing and referencing skills. Many homework problems are worked over the course of the semester in order to learn a new skill or technique. Practice (and failing at being "perfect") is an essential part of the learning process.

This need to fail is also part of the assessment process. As departments and units measure student learning outcomes, it is possible that not all outcomes are met at the level desired. Rather than viewing this as a bad event, departments and institutions should view this as an opportunity to make modifications to what they do. Assessment is a process that should give a better understanding of what is done well and, more important, what is not done well. Knowing where outcomes are not fully met allows that information to be better used to make informed decisions about what to focus on in the next academic year.

2

Transformative Assessment

A Historical Perspective

To paraphrase Hermann Ebbinghaus, assessment has a short history but a long past. Like Ebbinghaus's field of psychology, assessment has conceptually been occurring for hundreds, and perhaps thousands, of years. "The intellectual roots of assessment as a scholarship extend back well before its emergence as a recognizable movement" (Ewell, 2002a, p. 3). As a concept, assessment is simple: knowing what students should learn, discovering what they actually did learn, and then using that information to modify what is done to encourage learning. The complexity to the process comes with the layers of knowledge and the measurement of these layers. Assessment may be simple, but it is not easy.

Precursors to the Assessment Movement

According to Pat Hutchings and Ted Marchese (1990), students in the nineteenth century had to show the public that they had actually learned what they were supposed to have learned. "A candidate for the bachelor's, therefore, faced a final hurdle of the senior declamation . . . often these examinations were conducted orally, by and before outsiders" (p. 27). As Hutchings and Marchese point out, separating teaching from the evaluation of learning was important. The evaluation of learning was also something that could be demonstrated to interested and relevant constituencies. Currently, of course, accreditation visitors would not publicly question a student about what she knew, but it is not unheard of for the accreditation process to involve inspection of student work products that were used in the assessment process.

In the late eighteenth and early nineteenth centuries, more undergraduate students came to an increasingly larger number of institutions. A college degree became something that was given following the fulfillment of a set of agreed-on courses rather than an overall knowledge of an area. Hutchings and Marchese (1990) highlight the fact that in 1911, Harvard president A. L. Lowell addressed the Association of American Universities on the topic, "Disadvantages of the Current American Practice of Conferring Degrees (with the exception of the Ph.D.) on the Accumulation of Credits in Individual Courses, Rather Than as the Result of Comprehensive Examinations upon Broad Subjects."

Many working in higher education in the United States proceeded to develop innovations and create exciting change during the first quarter of the twentieth century. In 1935 a survey demonstrated that 252 colleges required a senior comprehensive exam (in 1925, that number was only 71; Hutchings & Marchese, 1990). But as numbers of students and institutions continued to rise, the percentage of students who were required to sit for a comprehensive exam within the major fell dramatically. "It has been many decades since the comprehensive examining of seniors placed a significant role in the award of degrees. In losing that practice, we lost as well a tradition of asking questions about our graduates' competence and about the cumulative effects of our teaching and curricula" (Hutchings & Marchese, 1990, p. 15).

In the mid-twentieth century, several areas emerged that demonstrated the need to gather information about student learning and development in higher education (Ewell, 2002a, 2002b). Arthur Chickering's work (1969) is still cited today as an important step in understanding college students' psychosocial development process. This work, followed by research by Alexander Astin (1977) and Pascarella and Terenzini (1991), led to a much better understanding of the concept of a long-term, value-added approach to studying student learning. At approximately the same time, studies on college student retention become increasingly meaningful (Ewell, 2002b). Together with Tinto's work (1975) on academic and social integration, a new way of looking at the importance of student learning, development, and behavior was established. This longitudinal approach to discovery led to specific models that are still used today. In addition, institutions recognized the necessity of tracking and increasing retention. This was a measure that was relatively easy to use, and it quickly became a benchmark for looking across institutions.

Program evaluation become more widely used in the 1960s, and according to Peter Ewell (2002a), early "program evaluation relied largely on quantitative methods" (p. 5). Much of the data collected for these program evaluation studies were surveys and cost-benefit analyses. Early program evaluations often focused on how students viewed particular programs; thus, satisfaction surveys become popular as a means to gather data. Because cost-benefit analyses were often a part of program evaluation, this view of an education program being "worth" what it was costing the university became an important variable. Because of what Peter Ewell calls "systems thinking," there was a need in program evaluation to look across a particular program rather than looking at the success of a single student.

The approach of mastery learning focused on the single student and what she or he had learned. The mastery learning concept was introduced in the American public schools in the 1920s with the work of Washburne (1922, cited in Block, 1971). Mastery learning was popular during the 1920s, but it was often time-consuming and difficult to do given the amount of time that had to be spent on an individual student. However, in the mid-twentieth century, the concept of mastery learning was brought back because of changes in technology. This newer form of mastery learning was called "programmed instruction" and was often able to provide students with the educational materials needed to allow them to move at their own pace while getting constant feedback on their correct and incorrect responses. During the 1960s, Bloom's article, "Learning for Mastery" (1968), helped bring mastery learning forward as an important pedagogical tool for public school education. While mastery learning has been more focused on elementary and secondary students, the concepts of mastery learning have made their way into higher education philosophy. Evergreen State University, Alverno College, and Antioch College, for example, demonstrate how mastery learning provided the partial foundation to the development of "alternative" institutions of higher education (Ewell, 2002a). In addition, "mastery methods posed an effective alternative to the prominent (and politically popular) 'testing and measurement paradigm' that is still used today" (p. 6).

In addition to the areas of college student development, retention initiatives, program evaluation, and mastery learning, another area has had an impact on the concept of transformative assessment: teaching and learning. When faculty teach, they also in many cases measure student learning. Some of this measurement is summative (exams, completed papers, or final presentations, for example). But some of the teaching/learning process occurs within the context of a single classroom moment: the faculty member makes a statement or draws a conclusion and, looking around, sees confused looks on student faces. Knowing that students have missed this point, the faculty member goes back and tries to explain in a different way. Then, seeing knowing looks of comprehension, he or she moves on to another topic. The cycle of assessment has been used (if not always documented) at almost every teaching and learning moment. Good faculty are regularly assessing student learning and using that information to enhance the course (sometimes in the moment of teaching, sometimes in ways that modify the course for the next time that it is taught). The teaching and learning process, when done fully, uses the assessment process to monitor student learning and improve the teaching process.

Given these areas that are often considered to be precursors to the current assessment movement, it is understandable that there is often confusion and disagreement regarding what the term *assessment* actually means. "More significantly, their values and methodological traditions are frequently contradictory, revealing conceptual tensions that have fueled assessment discussions ever since. . . . What is surprising in retrospect is that such disparate scholarly traditions could be related at all and that they continue to inform such a lively scholarship" (Ewell, 2002a, pp. 6–7).

Challenges to Integrating Assessment into Higher Education

Given the multipronged history of assessment, it is little wonder that it has not easily moved into the mainstream of higher education. But what has been striking about the development of higher education assessment has been the sometime vehement dislike and distrust of assessment. The challenges of creating a culture of assessment have been large. It is as if there needs to be a paradigm shift in terms of meaningfully assessing student learning at the department and institutional levels if transformative assessment is going to work. Several variables seem to be working against this potential paradigm shift, and it is important to understand the impact of each of these variables on the perception of assessment.

Definitions

The word *assessment* has several very different meanings. To the general public and those in counseling or special education, assessment is a diagnostic tool used to identify a particular problem within an individual patient, student, or client. For many college faculty, the concept of assessment focuses on a type of comprehensive evaluation, usually summative in nature. Bernard Madison (2001) has lamented the "burden of a name" that assessment must carry. He further states that faculty know "as did every farmer, that weighing one's produce did not hasten its readiness for market" (para. 2). The evaluative use of assessment has been a major challenge to using transformative assessment as a tool for enhancing learning because it focuses on demonstrating success in a summative way.

Peter Ewell likens another related definition of *assessment* to that used by mastery learning, "where assessment referred to the processes used to determine an individual's mastery of complex abilities" (Ewell, 2002a, p. 9). This focus is on assessment of individual student work. More recently, large-scale testing of K–12 students has been widely used for summative evaluation of schools and school districts. These statewide assessment programs are designed to compare school and district performance across the state. Clearly this type of assessment is focused on accountability, and, because of the No Child Left Behind Law passed in 2002 (Public Law 107–110), all states are required to participate in statewide testing. *Assessment* is a term that has clearly struggled with acceptance and use:

> We distinguished between summative assessment and formative assessment to try to clarify why assessment is done. We resorted to assessment cycles to imply that assessment was a continuous process rather than a discrete event. We added prepositional phrases to clarify the purpose when we talked of assessment of student learning and assessment in the service of learning . . . but the noun, and hence the center of attention, is assessment, and this word continues to convey misleading meanings and images in spite of modifying words or phrases [Madison, 2001, para. 3].

Assessment, then, is misunderstood by many who are mandated to perform it. And this becomes the crux of the problem: it is impossible to "do" assessment if the belief of what is done is incorrect or is only part of what needs to happen. Thus, the calls for closing the feedback loop became louder because data were collected (evaluation was completed) but never used.

Conceptual Understanding of Assessment

If it is true that many within higher education have such differing definitions of what assessment is and should be that it becomes difficult for a department-wide (much less nationwide) discussion about how to complete the assessment cycle as mandated. While it is certainly true that both accountability and enhancement of student learning are important aspects of assessment, it is crucial to come to agreement about the core purpose. "Though accountability matters, learning still matters most" (Angelo, 1999, p. 3).

Assessment as a practice in higher education seems as if it is here to stay: "Assessment thus has become an unavoidable condition of doing business: institutions can no more abandon assessment than they can do without a development office" (Ewell, 2002a, p. 22). Federal funding, national interest, and the push for accountability ensure that the practice of assessment will continue for many years to come. However, if the concept of assessment is still based on the need for accountability, higher education will never fully benefit from the knowledge that a meaningful assessment program can provide.

Results from several research studies provoke much thought about how assessment is conceptualized. Sixty-nine percent of institutions participating in the National Inventory of Institutional Support for Student Assessment indicated that preparing for accreditation was a major purpose for focusing on student assessment. "This study suggests that whereas excellence in undergraduate education is often stressed in an institution's mission (82%), a focus on student outcomes (52%) is less often mentioned and student assessment as an institutional priority (19%) is usually not included" (Peterson & Vaughan, 2002, p. 33). Higher education is not yet making the explicit connection between the stated desire for excellence and the necessary measures to continually enhance learning.

Assessment must be viewed as a means to regularly provide information about student learning that can be used to inform decision making and provide evidence to external constituencies that an institution is doing a good job. Unfortunately the accountability aspect (which is tied to funding, in many cases) has been the most visible purpose of assessment on most campuses. Moving toward a paradigm of transformative assessment is vital if higher education is to truly benefit from the resources put into the assessment movement.

An area of great difficulty in moving from accountability-driven assessment to transformative assessment is that of developing outcomes that are meaningful and rich but still measurable. Tom Angelo (1999) argues that "most assessment efforts have resulted in little learning improvement because they have been implemented without a clear vision of what 'higher' or 'deeper' learning is and without an understanding of how assessment can promote such learning" (pp. 3–4). Writing outcomes that reflect the complexity of learning is a difficult process and most likely will never be perfect. But because what is measured becomes what is valued, it is essential that learning outcomes be meaningful and important rather than easily quantified.

Developing outcomes is a process that must start with the mission statement of the institution or the departmental unit. The mission should be a broad, far-reaching, and descriptive statement that establishes the culture and purpose of the institution or department. Once the overall mission statement is widely accepted, it should provide the root for all other unit mission statements. Learning outcomes, then, should align with the mission statement and focus on the skills, content knowledge, beliefs, and values gained from participating in a specific program or course. Added to that, learning outcomes should also be measurable. This is often the most difficult part of assessment: creating meaningful *and* measurable outcomes that are rich enough to provide useful data and specific enough to give accurate data.

One error that often occurs during creation or modification of an assessment plan is that measures are decided on prior to the identification of learning outcomes. Measures are easy to discuss, and there are many that are commercially created, administered, and scored. But if the measure is not specific to the learning outcomes and mission statement of the institution or unit, its validity is compromised.

Quality Instruments

In a transformative assessment program, the mission and learning outcomes will be unique to that specific program or institution. Thus, in most cases, commercially available instruments were probably designed for another purpose. In the mid-1980s, testing companies created many new tests designed to measure student learning based on some common student learning outcomes. Thus, tests such as the Educational Test Services' Academic Profile and Major Field Achievement Tests became widely used. Other published instruments designed to measure student development, expectations regarding college life, and satisfaction with the institution were created and are still being used; examples are the Cooperative Institutional Research Program, the National Survey of Student Engagement, and the College Student Experiences Questionnaire. More recently, commercially available tests have been created to measure difficult constructs. For example, the Collegiate Learning Assessment measures critical thinking, analytical reasoning, and problem-solving skills. Although these types of published instruments can be good choices, they will provide appropriate information only if the outcomes are consistent with what is actually measured by the instrument.

Many institutions and departments are creating home-grown assessment instruments that measure specific outcomes for the program. From a transformative assessment perspective, this provides the opportunity to make a clear alignment from the mission to the outcomes and through to the measures. There are two methods for gathering information using in-house developed instruments.

One common way of gathering information is by adding the measurement to existing degree program requirements. A department might require that students take a senior-level comprehensive exam before they can graduate. Or all graduating seniors might be required to complete a portfolio including specific information gathered during their past four years. Satisfaction or alumni surveys are often used to gain information about specific learning outcomes.

A second way to get assessment information is to use embedded items that are already being used within specific courses. These are usually direct measures of student learning that have been used to measure an individual student's level of knowledge. In other words, the student work was used in calculating that student's grade. This course-level work can also be used to measure across students in a course or a department in order to assess a particular student outcome. For example, in a freshman English composition course, students are asked to write several types of papers and submit them for grading. Any one of those assignments could also be used to determine levels of writing ability or critical thinking skills.

When a course item also serves as an assessment measure, the institution typically uses a clean, or blind, copy of the student work because the student grade may or may not reflect whether that particular student has met a specific outcome. In an English composition course, for example, the student may have received a C grade because of grammar problems. But if that same paper is also used to measure critical thinking in a departmental assessment program, the student might have clearly met the outcome. The same holds true if a department is using a portfolio measure to look at student skills. Using a copy of the student work without the student name or any instructor comments allows the student work to be read solely for the purpose of assessing whether the departmental-level outcome has been met.

Accreditation Mandates

The word *accredit* is derived from the Latin word *credere*, which means "to trust." Accreditation is a voluntary system and is not directly supervised by the government, and it is based on trust. Accreditation organizations trust that the information given by individual institutions is correct and truthful. "Members of the higher education community would be wise to keep this trust in mind as they perform self-evaluations, because the alternatives could be much more difficult and not as effective in achieving quality improvement" (Alstate, 2004, p. 10). In order for the accreditation system to work, the integrity of the process must be upheld.

Accreditation formally became a "national phenomenon" in August 1906 (Alstete, 2004, p. 7). The National Association of State Universities met August 3–4, 1906, in order to create some set of standards for admission into postsecondary institutions (Young, Chambers, & Kells, 1983). The accreditation movement has certainly changed quite a bit in the past hundred years. In the mid-1980s, accreditation began to require that institutions focus on student learning outcomes rather than standards of higher education (Ratcliff, Lubinescu, & Gaffney, 2001; Alstete, 2004). "Prior to the 1980s, accreditation standards focused largely on processes, procedures, and the inputs that were supposed to result in educated, well-prepared students" (Davenport, 2001, p. 67). Since that time, all accredited institutions have been required to put into place a method for assessing student learning outcomes and a demonstrated use of the findings from their assessment plans. Most likely assessment would not be a widespread practice on campuses today if it had not been mandated by the regional accreditation organizations.

Accreditation in the United States began to focus on quality of student learning in the 1990s (Alstete, 2004). "Assessment and accreditation are both premised on the importance of quality assurance. Everyone in the educational enterprise has responsibility for maintaining and improving the quality of services and programs" (Ratcliff, Lubinescu, & Gaffney, 2001, p. 17). As regional accreditors begin to require documentation of quality efforts, institutions have responded by creating "quality enhancement plans" or an "academic quality improvement program," with the exact title depending on the regional accreditor's requirements. It is obvious that when accreditation standards and principles change, individual institutions must make modifications to meet the new requirements.

Assessment for Accountability

The concept of assessing for accountability is one of the reasons that assessment has not become more useful in higher education. Assessing for accountability focuses on the need to provide information to others—usually those who are external to the institution. Accreditation boards are an excellent example of how assessment for accountability is viewed. With this concept, assessment is done for others rather than for the purpose of enhancing learning within an institution. Assessment for accountability often is seen as a mandated process for which the institution must demonstrate that it has done well. If, to use reaccreditation visits as an example, an institution does not have a successful site visit, the institution could be put on some type of probation or have its accreditation status revoked, which has all kinds of negative effects. No institution wants to lose its accreditation status.

In the past, when an upcoming accreditation visit loomed, institutions would go into a frenzy of activity to prepare for the (usually) unwelcome visit. Everything would be shined and polished. If anything demonstrated that the institution had a problem, it was often hidden or written in a way to describe it as less damaging than it might actually be. This practice of showing only the good and not sharing the institution's ineffective areas, however, did not work to the advantage of the institution, its faculty, or its students.

The truth is that assessing only for the purpose of accountability leads to a punishment mentality. Thinking of assessment as a punishment rather than as an opportunity to gain information leads to a lot of wasted time and resources. Assessment only for accountability is likely to create a situation where assessing student learning outcomes is done right before the data are needed, and the data that are collected are chosen to demonstrate that the institution is doing well. The dirty laundry is ignored—and thus stays dirty. Fears about negative consequences resulting from the assessment process cause many to shy away from a serious, research-based inspection of student learning.

"The current political and social environment makes the topics of accountability and accreditation extremely important. Over the past two decades, state and federal governments have been emphasizing the need for some quality assurance and improvement mechanism for higher education" (Alstete, 2004, p. xi). There is a need for accreditation, and not just because of federal funding. Assessment for accountability will probably always be part of higher education (the process of demonstrating to an external audience what an institution is doing is important) not only for accreditation but also for the community, parents, and future students. Accountability is an important part of higher education, but it is not the only part, and it certainly is not the most important aspect of learning.

Assessment for Learning

All faculty assess student learning. By its very nature, the collegiate teaching and learning process encompasses measuring student learning. Faculty are very good at knowing what students have learned, and for the most part, they also usually are well aware of which students have not learned key information. Exams, papers, portfolios, and presentations are just some of the methods that faculty use to measure student learning.

Why, then, has it been difficult for many institutions to embrace the concept of assessment? Faculty assess student learning on a regular and ongoing basis. "Faculty should have access to a variety of outcomes measurements for student learning. While these may vary from department to department and institution to institution, the basic function is the same: information on how much and what type of learning students are gaining as a result of a course or program" (Wehlburg, 2004, p. 167). Assessment for learning is something that most instructors do well when considering the individual student.

Unfortunately it is probably because faculty, departments, and institutions have so many pieces of information regarding student learning that these are not often used in an overall assessment plan that looks across students and courses. Faculty are very good at assessing an individual student's learning, but often have more difficulty determining how to use a course-specific measure for a departmental-level assessment plan. However, the same items that are used in individual courses to determine a student's grade can also be used to look across students as part of an overall assessment tool.

Grades themselves, though, are not considered to be a good assessment measure of student learning. Although they are certainly representative of what an individual student learned in a specific course, they do not provide information that is used to look across students and determine what they learned and what they did not learn. For example, if a student receives a B in her Introduction to Psychology course, it is not known what she knows and does not know. That student may have done well on all but one section of the final exam, may have done B work all semester, or may have performed well on all of the content areas but missed some classes and lost points for those absences. This is why grades are not useful assessment measures. However, the student work that was used to determine the grade might be an excellent assessment tool. The final exam or the research paper for the course is a fine, direct measure of student learning. A review of these makes it much easier to determine what the student learned and, the more important question, what the student did not learn.

Assessment for Teaching

"Learning can and often does take place without the benefit of teaching . . . but there is no such thing as effective teaching in the absence of learning (Angelo & Cross, 1993, p. 3). Learning is, of course, the major goal of higher education, and the way that much of the planned learning occurs is through a course taught by an instructor. Students learn many things during their college time, but what is typically measured and meaningful to parents and future employers are the content and skills taught in the classroom. Assessment for teaching focuses on the tools to measure what students are learning so that the instruction can be modified to best ensure the desired quality of learning.

Classroom assessment techniques (CATs) are designed to provide an instructor information on what students are really learning. These CATs typically take a short time to provide useful information that can be used to inform teaching. A CAT should have the following characteristics (Angelo & Cross, 1993):

- It should be learner centered. Classroom assessment should focus on gathering information from observation and using that information to improve student learning. This is different from classroom observations that typically focus on the instructor's teaching but not on what the student is gaining. It is essential that the classroom assessment tool use what the students are demonstrating in terms of their learning, regardless of what the instructor is doing.

- It should be teacher directed. A classroom assessment tool should be chosen and used in a specific context. The "individual teacher decides what to assess, how to assess, and how to respond to the information gained through the assessment" (Angelo & Cross, 1993, p. 4). The purpose is to provide information to the instructor for her or his use.

- It should be mutually beneficial to both students and instructor. The classroom assessment technique, by its very nature, requires that students actively participate in the process. By doing this, "students reinforce their grasp of the course content and strengthen their own skills at self-assessment. Their motivation is increased when they realize that faculty are interested and invested in their success as learners" (Angelo & Cross, 1993, pp. 4–5).

- It should be formative in nature. The CAT is not designed to compare student work or to use it to see which students understand the material and which students do not. "The purpose of using classroom assessment techniques is to improve student learning—not to grade students' work" (Wehlburg, 2002, p. 189).

- It is context specific. CATs are designed to address a specific need within a specific course. Many variables will have an impact on what CAT is used: time available, size of the class, element of learning to be assessed, and even teacher personality.

- It should be ongoing. CATs are assessment practices, and therefore closing the feedback loop is important. "Instructors who use a variety of CATs over time and use that feedback to make appropriate changes, will find that students begin to participate more actively in the assessment process and in the class. After the first assessment and implementation of feedback, the instructor can use the same (or different) assessment again to check of the efficacy of the new/revised activity" (Wehlburg, 2002, p. 190).

- It should be rooted in good teaching practices. Using a CAT or a series of CATs can provide additional information to an instructor about what is working and what is not. "Teachers ask questions, react to students' questions, monitor body language and facial expressions, read homework and tests, and so on. Classroom assessment provides a way to integrate assessment systematically and seamlessly into the traditional classroom teaching and learning process" (Angelo & Cross, 1993, p. 6).

There are many forms of classroom assessment techniques, and most can be easily modified for a specific course or unit. Two of the most used are the Minute Paper and the Muddiest Point. An instructor who is using the Minute Paper asks students to respond briefly (in about one minute) to a specific probe. The probe might be general ("What was the most important thing that you learned in class today?"), or it might be specific ("Using Skinner's reinforcement theory, describe what is happening when the fussing child is given candy in the grocery store by the mother"). Asking students to respond on paper and then collecting the student writing, an instructor can get a lot of rich information about what elements of class were learned and which items need further discussion.

The Muddiest Point is similar to the Minute Paper in that it does not require much time to administer. This technique consists of asking students to respond to one question: "What was the muddiest point in today's class?" By gathering this information, the instructor can see if there is a set of responses from students indicating areas that need additional explanations or another set of reading.

There are hundreds of CATs available—Angelo and Cross (1993) describe fifty in detail—and some are designed to be used in an online setting. These CATs (often called techno-CATs) are classroom assessment tools that use some type of technology.

By gathering assessment information about student learning, an instructor can use the information to enhance teaching. This assessment for teaching should be an ongoing, formative, and cyclical process and can become an important part in an overall transformative assessment process.

Transformative Assessment

Transformative assessment should be appropriate, meaningful, sustainable, flexible, and ongoing, and it should use data for improvement with the potential for substantive change. In addition, the transformative assessment process must exist within a culture that expects the results to be important and useful. Tom Angelo (1999) has outlined four pillars of transformative assessment.

The first is to build shared trust. Trust is essential if change is going to occur. "The point is not to start with problems and debate, but by helping participants feel respected, valued, safe, and in the company of worthy peers" (Angelo, 1999, p. 5). Faculty must trust that their colleagues will listen to and respect their thoughts. More important, they must feel that when issues arise that indicate a need for change, colleagues will support that change and not try to remember an error when time for tenure or promotion arrives. Faculty also need to trust their department chairs, deans, and upper administration and know that the expectation is that there are areas that are not as strong as others. The success of transformative assessment is dependent on finding out what is not working as well as is hoped and then focusing on the areas in most need of enhancement. The administration must trust that the faculty will participate fully in the process of identifying outcomes, measurements, and in the analysis and use of the findings.

Second, according to Angelo, it is essential to build shared motivation: "Collectively identify goals worth working toward and problems worth solving—and consider the likely costs and benefits" (p. 5). By ensuring that all members of the institutional or departmental community have consensus about the overall goals and outcomes of the process, the chances increase that assessment will be a tool for enhancing student learning, faculty teaching, and even campus morale. When one institution began to develop a mechanism for assessing its core curriculum, a great deal of time was first spent on discussions about the process and on how all involved would have a voice and a vote. This made the start-up begin a little more slowly, but by the end of the multiyear process, the consensus building had created the opportunity for real change.

The third of Angelo's pillars is to build a shared language: "Building a shared vision for transformative change requires shared mental models and shared language for describing and manipulating those models" (p. 6). For example, if one of the outcomes that will be developed focuses on critical thinking, it is essential that all involved understand what is meant by that term. Sometimes institutions develop shorthand mechanisms for referring to a particular topic. What one campus might call general education, another might call "the core." It does not matter what the agreed-on definitions are, just that everyone involved understands what they mean.

And finally, build shared guidelines. What criteria or principles are important? How will the individuals know that the institution is moving in the right direction? Knowing the answers to these questions and developing these answers regarding assessment will help to keep the process open, transparent, and transformative. Richard Shavelson (2007a) cautions against the use of narrow assessment measures that do not reflect the rich context of higher education when he states that an institution should "do this assessing in a coherent system that measures the broad spectrum of outcomes, for, if this is not done, the system's output measures will become the narrow outcome measures of higher education" (p. 23). A process of transformative assessment will give higher education the information that it needs to identify the areas that can and should be changed. There are certainly challenges to overcome, but by learning from history, innovative and meaningful change will take place.

3

Institutional Dynamics
Using Organizational Structure and Campus Climate

Transformational assessment, by its very nature, is not something that can be done using cookie-cutter approaches. By definition, transforming a campus is done in a unique and specific way because that individual institution has a particular mission, history, values, and sense of what is important. The role of transformative assessment therefore must take into consideration several aspects of the campus. However, there are aspects to any institution that are not unique. Accreditation demands, the role of national rankings, and budget concerns are often similar. These cross-institutional areas of concern must also be included if a transformative assessment process is going to work.

Traditional Concerns of Faculty

"I have never met a faculty member who was excited about doing assessment, although rumor has it they exist" (Berheide, 2007, p. 27). Ralph Wolf and Olita Harris (1994) have described stages that an institution typically goes through with regard to assessment. These stages are based on the work by Elizabeth Kübler-Ross's stages of death and dying (use of this theory when discussing assessment is often seen as humorous by many faculty).

Mary J. Allen (2004) has characterized typical faculty and departmental responses for each stage:

- Denial—"It's a fad. If I ignore it, it will go away."
- Acceptance—"Okay, I guess we have to do it."
- Resistance—"I feel threatened. My department feels threatened. My campus feels threatened. Can I subvert it by not participating in the process or in some other way?"
- Understanding—"Maybe we can learn something useful. Can we use what we've already been doing?"
- Campaign—"We have a plan. Maybe it's not perfect, but let's get moving!"
- Collaboration—"We have a plan with long-range objectives that are clearly defined, and based on our experience with assessment, we believe it works."
- Institutionalization—"We can't imagine working without assessment. It's a permanent part of our institutional culture." (p. 7)

Moving from the denial stage into one where the institution values and uses assessment data as part of an overall effectiveness process is crucial if a campus is going to boost the quality of its educational outcomes. However, this is not an easy paradigm shift. It takes a great deal of time, trust, and work to institutionalize transformative assessment. Typically faculty see several barriers blocking the possibility of their buying in to the full assessment process.

Time

In his presidential address to the 2003 Eastern Sociological Society meeting, Jerry Jacobs (2004) acknowledged that faculty work hard and have little time for many thing outside academia.

Jacobs indicated that "aquatic references" are often used: "I am swamped at the moment" or "I'm under water," or "I'm drowning in (papers, exams, proposals, committee work)" (p. 3). Life within academia, family time, community involvement, and relaxation all add up to large numbers of hours. Many of these hours are spent at their university, and faculty are not often likely to agree to add hours there to their already full day. During the workday, faculty teach, provide service, spend time researching and writing, and often advise students individually or within a student organization.

According to the 2006 Faculty Survey of Student Engagement (FSSE), full-time faculty allocate about 60 percent of their time to teaching-related activities (for example, time in class and grading), 15 percent of their time to research and scholarly activities, and 25 percent of their time to other activities such as advising and service. As this total equals 100 percent of time, it is easy to see why adding assessment responsibilities to the faculty workload is problematic. Most faculty simply do not have time to work on an assessment project, especially if that project is not valued by colleagues or even the greater institution. Since by definition, faculty workload is already at 100 percent, any additional assessment work will have to be placed within another already existing category of faculty load.

In theory, assessment activities might fall under the service heading at many institutions. However, there is usually not a large amount of time that is already devoted to service, and much of that might be already taken up with departmental or institutional committee work or service to the community or the profession. In addition, service is not something that gets counted at many institutions toward promotion or tenure activities.

Another area that assessment activities might be logically placed within a faculty member's workload is that of scholarship. Developing and measuring student learning outcomes could be considered scholarly activity and might be information that could be submitted for publication. Again, however, the way that this type of scholarship is used to reward faculty in terms of promotion and tenure varies widely from institution to institution.

The final category as indicated by the 2006 FSSE data is that of teaching activities. It is quite possible that assessment activities, especially those that use student work products from specific courses, could also be done under the umbrella topic of teaching activities.

The issue of faculty time is not the same for all faculty members. Typically junior faculty spend less time on service and more time preparing for courses that they have not taught before. In addition, they are more likely to be spending a large amount of time in developing or more clearly defining a research track that they hope will eventually lead to tenure. In the light of this situation, many might consider that senior faculty may have more time to spend on assessment activities. But this is not always the case. Often junior faculty are asked to take on the tasks that have already cycled through the senior faculty or do the things that no one else wants to do. According to research by Marcia Bellas and Robert Toutkoushian (1999), junior faculty spent more time performing service activities than their higher-ranked colleagues did. If newer tenure-track faculty are asked to do a higher percentage of service (including assessment activities), those junior faculty members may be placed in a bind. There is certainly the time commitment problem, but there is also the difficulty of perhaps seeing that things might be done differently with assessment within the department. This may not sit well with senior faculty who have known assessment to be something strictly for accountability and therefore not a useful activity.

Institutions looking to modify existing assessment planning and processes to incorporate their use for transformation may face difficulty in moving to this new paradigm. Change is often hard, and shifting from the attitude of "but we've always done it this way" can be a challenge that many junior faculty may not be able to politically face. In order for faculty to accept and buy into the use of assessment for transformational purposes, it is essential to acknowledge the time that these new or modified processes will take. And tied to this is the potential that the work done in assessment could also benefit other existing categories of faculty time.

Scholarship

In 1990, Ernest Boyer's *Scholarship Reconsidered* changed the way that educators thought about the concept of scholarship. Prior to Boyer's book, many considered research, the discovery of new knowledge, as the primary and most often recognized form of scholarship. Boyer, however, conceptualized research as representing only a single form of scholarship and identified the areas of application, integration, and teaching as scholarship as well.

In 1997, Charles Glassick, Mary Huber, and Gene Maeroff proposed a model that could be used to evaluate all forms of scholarly activity. This model outlined six criteria that could be used to evaluate any form of scholarship: clarity of goals, adequacy of preparation, appropriateness of methods, significance of results, effectiveness of presentation, and reflective critique. This evaluation model has become important because it shows that all forms of scholarship can be assessed in similar ways.

Moving from assessing to other forms of scholarship, Trudy Banta (2002) has delineated "scholarly assessment"—that is, assessment "aimed at improving the day-to-day conduct of assessment" (p. x)—and "the scholarship of assessment," which is systematic inquiry designed to deepen and extend the foundation of knowledge underlying assessment" (p. x). Some faculty may not be interested in the scholarship of assessment, but they may in fact be willing to focus some of their scholarship time on determining how much and why students within their disciplines may be learning. In addition, faculty may develop a test or survey instrument and then, after seeing the results, decide if a modification in "the next iteration would produce a more desirable set of data to guide improvement in the future" (T. Banta, personal communication, February 19, 2007).

In departmental assessment strategies, there should be some mechanism for measuring student learning against a particular set of student learning outcomes. When a department discovers and documents in its assessment plan that its students are improving their learning, they should be encouraged and supported in developing discipline-specific manuscript presentations using these data. A number of teaching-related journals are refereed, and many of these will probably "count" for the tenure and promotion process. Institutions should consider methods to support faculty who use exciting assessment results in their research that demonstrate pedagogies that work to enhance learning.

Teaching

College campuses have data on student learning. Almost every course that is taught asks students to demonstrate what has been learned. There are papers, projects, exams, quizzes, and many other forms of student learning data. These items are designed to measure an individual student's knowledge of a particular concept with a course that exists within the setting of a department. And in most cases, that is the only purpose for the student assignment. But these course-based collections of student work can and should be used for departmental assessment information. Clearly a sample of student papers from a capstone course, for example, could be used to look across students within the department to determine how well the department is meeting a particular set of outcomes. Thus, student work can be used for two reasons: to grade the student and to assess student learning across a department. However, not all faculty are willing to undertake the analysis of student work from a colleague's class, and not many want to spend the time that good-quality assessment takes. "While all professors take responsibility for creating and disseminating knowledge, most do not like to be held accountable for whether their students master it" (Cutler, 2006, p. 69).

It is clear that information from individual courses can be used to assess student learning across a department. But information should flow not only from these individual courses into the departmental assessment plan. Information that is discovered at the department level can and should inform decisions that individual faculty members make about specific courses. For example, if data from an alumni survey indicate that recent students did not gain sufficient teamwork skills, this information can be used to modify an existing course by adding course activities that not only focus on content but also add teamwork or group learning skills.

When faculty see how assessment data can be used in their courses, they may see additional value working to collect or analyze that data. Faculty teaching time might be viewed as well spent in assessment activities when the result is a stronger course. The key is to ensure that student learning outcomes data are not used in punishing ways. If, for example, it is determined that students do not have the expected levels of knowledge and that content is taught in only one course, the faculty member teaching that course might receive lower merit increases or be at risk for not gaining tenure status. Transformative assessment activities should focus more on enhancing and modifying curricular and other structures than on punishing those who are viewed as not doing a good enough job. This type of assessment is an opportunity to move forward in a transparent and agreed-on way, not a means to weed out faculty.

Scott Cottrell and Elizabeth Jones (2002) interviewed faculty to determine their expectations for student learning, types of pedagogies used, how they evaluated student learning, and how they used those assessment results in their courses. They also analyzed the learning outcomes listed on the syllabi from these faculty members' courses and found that "participating faculty members used assessment findings to make deliberate and informed changes in their course designed to maximize student learning and development" (p. 7).

Service

To many faculty, the concept of service means having to serve on yet another committee that will eat up a great deal of time that takes away from their focus on research and teaching (Berberet, 1999). But history shows that as early as the mid-1600s, faculty were often tutors (Ward, 2003). Martin Finkelstein (1984) looked at academic life from three angles. The first is that faculty life is focused on the "disciplinary career": knowledge of specific content and subject matter. The second is that of the "institutional career," where their activities are associated with their own institution. The institutional career might focus, for example, on issues related to moving through the tenure system. Finally, Finkelstein focuses on the "external career," where the focus is on activities related to their work and require professional expertise but are done outside the institution, for example, community consulting, public lecturing, or other forms of public service.

During the eighteenth and nineteenth centuries, instructors were responsible not only for the disciplinary-based intellectual growth of their students but also for their moral and spiritual development. According to Finkelstein (1984), faculty were to be both teachers and "shepherds" to their students. As institutions have moved forward in the twenty-first century, there is still debate over the roles of teaching, research, and service. "In spite of the universality of higher education's mission and the work of faculty to provide 'teaching, research, and service,' the service dimension of faculty roles remains vaguely defined, unevenly distributed, poorly rewarded, and intellectually disconnected from the former two" (Berberet, 1999, p. 32).

Even with this disconnect regarding faculty roles, there is still the belief that service is part of each faculty member's job description. Anna Neumann and Aimee LaPointe Terosky (2003) "define service as faculty members' contributions to the (a) governance, management, and operation of their employing institution in whole or in part, internally and externally; (b) the work of their professional/disciplinary associations; and (c) the maintenance of their disciplines and fields at large" (p. 282). Assessment activities could be seen as part of this definition in terms of both focusing on the accreditation needs of the institution and maintaining and learning about student knowledge within the disciplinary field.

Most postsecondary institutions now have an active and ongoing assessment program that involves campuswide and department-based committees. This activity often focuses around the needs for accountability, but there is another option: this same amount of faculty time and energy could be used for asking questions that will give information about student learning that can make a transformational difference to the department and institution.

As an outcome of their participation in service activities (including assessment committees), faculty may find that the networking and information they gain has future potential. "At times, engagement in service contributed to study participants' scholarly learning in less direct but nonetheless powerful ways: it brought new sources of substantive knowledge—in the form of new colleagues—their way" (Neumann & Terosky, 2003, p. 296).

Issues in Current Higher Education

Several ongoing and widespread issues affect decision making across institutions of higher education. Assessment, accreditation, and national rankings are issues that each administration on almost every campus has to pay attention to in order to be successful. Unfortunately, many institutions see these as things that are "done to" a campus. In reality, assessment is something that should be done for transformation, and this can shape what occurs in the reaccreditation process. National rankings, however, seem often to be virtually unchangeable by the institution. However, all three of these areas can influence the ways in which an individual institution is viewed by others.

Assessment

It is difficult to read any higher educational journal or attend a higher education conference that does not mention the need for and the use of assessment. Assessment issues are so closely tied to accountability and accreditation that it is often difficult to separate them when the discussion occurs at the overall institutional level. Consider the report by the secretary of education's Commission on the Future of Higher Education, which laments "a lack of clear, reliable information about the cost and quality of postsecondary institutions, along with a remarkable absence of accountability mechanisms to ensure that colleges succeed in educating students" (U.S. Department of Education, 2006b, p. vii). Assessment should provide the evidence regarding student learning and the institution's role in promoting it.

Regardless of faculty interest, administrations, boards of trustees, and certainly governmental agencies are very interested in assessing student learning. Unfortunately this interest often takes the form of needing "proof" that acceptable levels of learning are happening. Assessment, then, takes the form of providing evidence of success to outside sources. No chancellor of a university would want to declare publicly that the institution had failed to meet the standards (outcomes) it had set for itself. So assessment is often seen as a tool for affirming only the positive learning outcomes. Unfortunately many of the outcomes that are part of the rich complexity of higher education are not easily measured. And if attempts to measure them do occur, it might be found that the institution has not been as successful as desired. Those focused on transformative assessment would find this exciting information: it would help to make decisions and put resources where a real difference could be made. But in many institutional cultures, this type of finding would be seen as problematic. Thus, many institutions view assessment activities as bean counting and confirming what is already known.

If higher education is going to continue to flourish and grow, it is imperative that measures be created that truly discover what is important and then use that finding to continuously hone the work of the individual institutions, departments, and faculty. Focusing on measurable but small pieces of student learning will never give the entire picture:

> Americans know that their world is being dramatically reshaped by scientific and technological innovations, increasing global interdependence and cross-cultural encounters, and a shifting balance of economic and political power. To succeed in this rapidly shifting environment, college graduates need a broader set of skills and knowledge. Today's graduates need to be intellectually resilient, cross-culturally literate, technologically adept, morally grounded, and fully prepared for a future of continuous and cross-disciplinary learning [Association of American College and Universities, 2006, para. 5].

Issues of assessment are not going to go away. Individuals within institutions and institutional representatives need to take responsibility for looking for methods to measure the complexities of higher education. Even if the measures are somewhat imperfect, striving to get at these multifaceted concepts is one of the first steps in gathering the data that can be used to make a meaningful difference.

Accreditation

According to the Council for Higher Education Accreditation (CHEA), accreditation is "the primary means of assuring and improving the quality of higher education institutions and programs in the United States (2006, para. 1). For over a century, regional accreditation bodies have accredited higher education institutions. This accreditation has certainly been tied to funding and thus is essential to most administrators. However, the need for accreditation has often been tied to funding and a need to "pass." Because of this, the lead-up time to many accreditation visits is a frenzy of preparation, often guided by the sense that only the positive aspects of a campus should be shown and the rest hidden. "The assessment process is often put off until the last possible moment, and then it can become a heavy and externally mandated load" (Wehlburg, 1999, p. 7). Also, the accreditation process is based on a set of standards that describe the minimum level of acceptable compliance. Many institutions are doing more than the minimum requirement, "making accreditation too often merely a compliance exercise" (Carey, 2007, p. 27).

Few administrators look forward to reaccreditation visits. They are seen, often at best, as a necessary hoop. However, the need to keep reaccreditation status is high on the list of issues important to upper-level university administrators. In fact, the role of accreditation is important and should be seen as a "collegial, yet rigorous, system of self study and peer review to examine and enhance their [the university's] teaching and learning, research, and service roles" (Eaton, 2007, p. 19). If accreditation is going to be a means for benefiting teaching and learning, as Eaton suggests, institutions must be more transparent in their self-studies and their preparations. The Southern Association of Colleges and Schools, Commission on Colleges (2006) states that "integrity, essential to the purpose of higher education, functions as the basic contract defining the relationship between the Commission and each of its member and candidate institutions. It is a relationship in which all parties agree to deal honestly and openly with their constituencies and with one another" (p. 6). This belief that integrity and honesty are essential in order for accreditation to work meaningfully is an important concept. Many institutions are not prepared to show potentially negative aspects of what they do. Yet a shift in thinking about accreditation is necessary if true change is going to occur. An institutional culture that defines itself by reflection on data and actively seeks out areas that could be improved will continue to evolve and improve. Kevin Carey (2007) acknowledges that the accreditation process now requires institutions to develop outcomes, measures of student learning, and to use the resulting information to make higher education a continuously improving system. "Historically they [accreditors] have put their emphasis on issues such as financial integrity and faculty governance. These things, while important, have little to do with teaching, knowledge creation, and other essential purposes of the university" (p. 27).

National Rankings

The largest-selling issue of *U.S. News & World Report* each year is the one on the rankings of U.S. colleges and universities. Boards of trustees and senior administration members often place a great deal of emphasis on these rankings. "Administrators wait with bated breath for them [the rankings] to arrive each fall and brag when their schools do well; trustees fret about them; campuses even hire independent consultants to help figure out how to game them" (Graham & Thompson, 2001, para. 14). *U.S. News & World Report* is not the only organization publishing information comparing institutions; *Peterson's Four Year Colleges* (Peterson's, 2008) and *The Insider's Guide to Colleges* (Yale Daily News Staff, 2008) are just a few of the many. However, the *U.S. News & World Report* rankings have caught the attention of many because they gather objective information about institutions that they use to make purportedly objective comparisons. Recently several institutions have chosen to have their institutional data excluded from these rankings. However, many potential college students and their parents read these rankings as they are considering college options. Not having an institution listed in this ranking system might be considered to hurt an institution's chances of having more student applications. But often the information that is reported in these national rankings uses only part of what might be used in making a college choice. And there is no guarantee that a student will have success at a particular institution just because most other students do. The difficulty is, of course, that the information collected does not tell a potential student or parent anything about how much a particular student might learn or even what that student might learn. Nevertheless, these rankings are taken very seriously. A study reported in the *Journal of College Admissions* found that "when an institution improved in the rankings, [with] other factors held constant . . . the next year it received more applications and could then accept a smaller fraction of these applications" (Ehrenberg, 2005, p. 30). Thus, rankings are seen as an essential admissions and marketing tool.

Primarily the information that goes into rankings are input-type variables—for example, an institution's reputation, amount of funding for faculty, and the achievement of its entering graduation class. None of these variables, however, can indicate what students actually learn when they get to that institution, and satisfaction with an institution (as measured by retention rates and alumni giving) is not a good measure of learning either.

Student learning is not directly considered in national rankings. However, other potential methods for ranking institutions could be based on student learning. The Collegiate Learning Assessment and the National Survey of Student Engagement are often mentioned as potential sources for rankable information that could be used. But just because something can be done does not necessarily mean that it should be done. Often the common denominator that is used to measure across institutions leaves out the richness and individuality of differing missions. All institutions do not hold the same belief systems, do not prioritize learning in the same ways, and should not be measured on only specific items that leave out their individuality.

National rankings will probably remain an important area for institutions (especially the senior-level administrators) for a very long time, even though some institutions have chosen not to submit data for inclusion in the rankings. But if these same senior administrators could also look for institution-specific measures of student learning, this information could help to focus what occurs on a campus, and the reactions to the national rankings may not be pushed into making modifications that have little impact on learning. "Five years ago, U.S. News introduced its category crediting schools for high alumni donation rates, a simple change which spawned scores of programs across the country where students call up alumni to ask for money. . . . Instead of encouraging students to talk to alumni for the sake of fund-raising, it could encourage faculty to talk to students for the sake of learning" (Graham & Thompson, 2001, para. 41).

Organizational Responsibility for Assessment

The role of assessment must move from a top-down mandated requirement to one that is focused on measuring student learning in order to improve student learning. Faculty are the ones who work with students on a daily basis and know what students are learning. They must be given the right and the responsibility for creating assessment plans that will result in appropriate and usable data. At many institutions, however, the assessment results required by departments are filed away. Rarely are departments asked what they are doing with the results. And the quality of outcomes, measures, and findings is something that is usually not closely inspected. It is often enough that outcomes, measures, and findings simply exist. But if an institution is to embrace the concept of transformative assessment, there must be an organizational structure in place that supports and rewards quality assessment work in the departments.

A single unit or person should be able to guide and understand what is happening in assessment across all institutional areas. At many institutions, a director of assessment organizes and plans assessment activities. This position should report to the provost or, better, the president or chancellor. Being able to use data from across campus (academic affairs, student affairs, alumni offices, and so forth) is crucial to the success of a sustainable assessment plan. The director of assessment should also know whom to contact in each department and unit so that although the actual planning and data gathering take place at the department level, there is institutional oversight. Good communication and a collegial atmosphere are essential if assessment is going to be built on trust and the knowledge that the data will be used to improve, not to punish. Support for the ongoing assessment planning and use of assessment data should be widespread and include the president or chancellor's office, the provost, deans, and department chairs. As part of this support, it is essential that the data gathered be used. Department chairs should use assessment results to support budget requests, deans should acknowledge assessment findings, and the institution should celebrate opportunities for positive change.

In response to a request from Trudy Banta, Tim Detwiler, dean of assessment and general studies at Cornerston University, developed a list of characteristics of an institutional assessment champion:

1. A respected member of the campus community (both for academics and student development).
2. Someone who is involved externally with the broader assessment movement—legitimizing his/her campus role.
3. A degreed member of the campus community.
4. One who is embedded in the campus culture (not seen as a "hired gun").
5. One who values a collegial decision-making process, desiring to influence change over time at the deepest institutional levels.
6. An individual who is able to work with people at multiple levels of the institution in multiple contexts.

7. Some who has a "stick-to-it" attitude.
8. Someone who is patient yet persistent.
9. Someone with access to support staff dedicated to the work of assessment [Banta, 2005, p. 15].

There are certain dimensions that can be used in order to determine how well an institution is doing with regard to using assessment as a transformative process. Washington State University (2003) has developed a reference guide in order to determine the level of transformative assessment. As part of this rubric, called "assessing transformation," institutions can place their own efforts on a Likert scale of 1 (Administrative) to 6 (Transformative). The rubric has these elements:

- Assessment purpose: The assessment plan aligns with other institutional plans and promotes a collaboration of administration, faculty, students, and community.

- Data acquisition and analysis: Data from multiple and diverse sources illuminate students' learning, learning processes, and learning purposes, particularly learning that extends beyond course-specific outcomes.

- Application of findings: The assessment findings are used to systematically inform and reshape teaching and learning practice in order to improve effectiveness, efficiency, and value, and specifically to promote an operational "culture of evidence" (for example, influence promotion and tenure decisions).

- Dissemination: Results are reported internally and externally with plans for expanding the collaboration for transformation.

As an institution works to organize its structure in ways that support the use of student learning data to enhance teaching and learning, it is important to regularly assess how well the institution is moving. Washington State University's guide can be useful for this purpose.

Planning and Budgeting Process

In theory, integrating the assessment process, planning, and budgeting makes a great deal of sense. Assessment efforts should bear on planning, and the planning process should guide the development of the budget. However, most institutions do not have a well-defined administrative structure that will allow this to happen. And when there is a lack of integration among these three important processes, often the budget drives the planning process, and the assessment data do not have much of an impact on either. "Planning cannot survive without a budget, neither planning nor budgeting can survive with integrity without assessment. And assessment is necessary to identify areas to target with quality principles that need to be planned and budgeted" (Griffith, Day, Scott, & Smallwood, 1996).

Clearly there is organizational need to link the assessment process with planning and budgeting. However, implementing this integration is difficult since the existing organizational structure may not easily incorporate the new collaborative efforts. Many institutions are working toward this integrative organization and have restructured in order to better use the assessment data in planning and budgeting. For example, the mission statement for the Indiana University-Purdue-University-Indianapolis (IUPUI) office for planning and institutional improvement is "to develop, integrate, and continuously improve institutional planning, implementation strategies, evaluation, and improvement activities at IUPUI." This office has integrated the planning and assessment process by working to provide information and resources to the campus community that will improve processes and outcomes. Also, the Butte Community College district in California uses a planning-budgeting-assessment process in which the assessment data inform the planning process, which in turn drives the budgeting process.

Methods for Creating a Climate for Transformational Assessment

Several crucial elements should be incorporated to modify the existing climate to one that embraces the concepts of transformative assessment.

The first is to engage faculty in the process. It is essential that a critical mass of faculty who care about assessment and student learning are involved from early in the process. Faculty need to see that transformative assessment is not something that is imposed on them; rather, it is something that is already being done within courses and whole departments. Identifying faculty who are already involved with some level of assessment is a good place to start. Departmental assessment liaisons or faculty involved with specialized accreditation within their disciplines are often excellent candidates. These are, however, the faculty members who are extremely busy within the institution.

Therefore, the institution must provide resources and support for those working on transformative assessment. This may often take the form of course release time, but faculty are also often willing to do additional work if other forms of support are given. Travel funds, undergraduate work-study students, or graduate student research support can be used to support this type of work. Faculty who can use their time working with assessment for other scholarly activities often participate too.

Once faculty are engaged and working toward the meaningful and appropriate use of data, it is imperative that the institution use the collected data. While this may seem like an obvious part in the process, too many institutions have binders, file cabinets, and CDs full of unused but excellent data focusing on student learning. As an institution moves toward a culture of using assessment for transformation, data collected early in the process must inform decision making. The senior administration must value the work done and the analysis of the data. Once the administration views the data as useful and meaningful, the chances that there will be a continuing need for the data become apparent, and those who are creating outcomes and measures will become essential to the process.

Transformative assessment rarely works well when only a small group of individuals has responsibility. Therefore, another element in moving toward an institutional culture that values this is to share the responsibility for assessment. Having an assessment office that can coordinate efforts is important, but the faculty who are participating in the effort must know that they drive the process. Faculty and departments must have the authority to create outcomes that they consider important, and they must be allowed to measure them in ways that are meaningful to them.

At Texas Christian University, the general education program is assessed by outcomes created and approved by the faculty through the faculty senate. The development of measures for these outcomes has been delegated to faculty who teach in the various areas. The assessment formats differ greatly across the general education curriculum, but all areas must submit their assessment findings at prescribed times. How the findings are generated, however, is completely up to the faculty groups with responsibility for that area. The result is a general education assessment program that reflects the complexity and richness of a liberal arts education.

Finally, in order for the institutional culture to begin to shift, it is vital to create a need. "You can't mandate a drive to improve, and all the tools in the world are beside the point if there's no sense that improvement is an urgent need. So where does the drive to do better come from? How can it be prompted? How does it get built into the culture?" (Hutchings, 1996, p. 8). The push for assessment on college campuses did not happen because individual institutions thought that gathering data on student learning was a good idea. Assessment became widespread because it was required for accreditation. This has been the initial push for measuring student learning at the departmental and institutional levels. If assessment is to move from a mandated process to one that is used and becomes meaningful to an institution, there must be some additional need. The external pressure for assessment will remain, but what is needed is an internal, intrinsic need for knowing what students are learning and focusing on changing what should be changed. The push this time must come from those who work the most with student learning: faculty. The need that already exists is the need to strengthen teaching and learning. For the most part, faculty know what and how much students know, and they use that information in their classes. But what has not happened is the use of those data to make departmental and institutional decisions. If this is to occur, an institutional structure must be in place that rewards increased student learning and emphasizes the need for high-quality assessment practices. Unfortunately, teaching quality is most often measured by end-of-semester course evaluations rather than direct measures of student learning. And while teaching may be rewarded at many institutions, the measure for quality is rarely based on student learning outcomes.

Institutional Dynamics

Transformative assessment is a process that will not suddenly appear on any college campus; it must grow from the ground up. And it is not something that can be easily mandated and done periodically for accreditation purposes. In fact, this transformative process already exists on almost all campuses. It might be done in a particular department or by faculty members who regularly use student learning as a tool to help revise a course. "Assessment is neither new nor exotic. It is and has been a part of every faculty member's work. All that is new is going beyond one class and one professor to ask the question 'Do you see?' over a broader range of material and probe further to find how learning can be improved" (Madison, 2001, para. 11).

In order to unleash the inspirational power of transformative assessment, institutions must recognize that this process takes time and that the time spent is valuable and worthwhile. Institutions must respect and use the information that comes from this process and ensure an openness to complex and ongoing discussions of learning and pedagogy. They must focus on the depth and richness of knowledge and how it might be measured without demanding that there be a single answer to any given question. Transformative assessment is a formative process that reiterates itself in a constantly improving cycle. When institutional dynamics are focused on what, how, and how much students are learning and less on demonstrating accountability, they will be moving in the direction of creating a true culture of learning.

4

Encouraging Faculty Support for Transformative Assessment

Typically when most faculty hear about "assessment" or "accountability" issues, they run away as quickly as they can. Many believe that these initiatives will soon go away just like many of the other educational and management fads. If this is the belief, then, it is little wonder that most faculty are not piling aboard the assessment wagon. Nevertheless, faculty support is essential. All of the assessment work, data collection, and reports will not have any bearing on higher education until those who are most closely involved with teaching and learning can use the data to make changes at the classroom level.

In an interview reported by Welsh and Metcalf (2003b), a faculty member stated, "I think most faculty see institutional effectiveness as a detraction from their jobs and a burden on them in terms of time and energy" (pp. 39–40). New programs or initiatives can be extremely productive and meaningful, but they will not be sustained until faculty support and leadership are in place. As the concept of assessment and accreditation moves from being simply resource based to a focus on outcomes, the knowledge necessary to design and implement assessment and institutional effectiveness activities must move into the hands of the faculty. "An outcomes-based approach cannot be pursued merely by documenting that the conditions necessary for quality educational experiences to take place are present. Today, institutions must demonstrate the impact of instruction on student learning and that faculty members are actually using the results of these assessments to improve instruction" (Welsh & Metcalf, 2003b, p. 450). Transformative assessment is, by definition, a participatory process. Faculty must support and lead in the development of the process, and in many cases, they must hold primary responsibility for analyzing and using the data gathered in the process.

In their research study, John Welsh and Jeff Metcalf (2003b) identified three areas that were crucial if faculty were going to support institutional effectiveness efforts. The first was that faculty perceived that the primary motivation for institutional effectiveness and assessment was improvement of the institution rather than accountability to others: "The regression analysis demonstrates the point that institutional improvement is a more compelling justification for institutional effectiveness than is responsiveness to external mandates" (p. 40). Second, individual faculty are likely to be more supportive of institutional effectiveness if they are personally involved with the planning and follow-through of specific activities. Finally, Walsh and Metcalf found that "outcomes-oriented" faculty (those who defined quality as how well students were learning) were more supportive of assessment and institutional effectiveness activities.

The relationship and the level of trust between faculty and the administration also can have an impact on how willing faculty are to take on new tasks. According to the Pew Higher Education Research Group (1996), when there is a philosophical separation between faculty and administration at an institution, usually less collaborative and collegial work is done in areas that require faculty and administrators to work together. Often administrators are asked to respond to several external forces, which might include alumni, the board of trustees, and the community. One of these external forces has been accrediting bodies. As accreditors have asked for additional work in institutional and departmental assessment, administrators have turned to faculty to focus on these areas. When faculty are asked to measure and account for student learning, many may feel that their work is being questioned: "Accountability entails measurement, in short, and that provokes academic resistance" (Ohmann, 2000, p. 6).

Nevertheless, it is crucial to have not only faculty support but faculty leadership as well if transformative assessment is going to be successful. Although several organizational factors must be in place, this chapter examines activities and services that can be provided to support faculty interest in assessment issues. Steve Crowe, director of the Higher Learning Commission of the North Central Association, said in testimony before the National Commission on Accountability in Higher Education that "we have greatly underestimated faculty acceptance of accountability and, consequently, have not tapped their creativity in defining and implementing meaningful systems for it" (Cumberland County College, 2005, p. 1). Faculty understanding and collaboration are essential if assessment is to be used for a transformative system.

Guidance for Writing Outcomes and Assessment Plans

Faculty regularly measure student learning. Each course contains several mechanisms for gathering evidence about what and how much students are learning. Most faculty are good at measuring what students know, but it is often difficult for them to translate their skills in measuring student learning for a course to using that same knowledge to develop departmental assessment plans. (See Exhibit 4.1.)

In a recent conversation among several faculty in one department, one said that assessment would never work because it was too subjective: "Student learning in our area can't be measured." Nevertheless, it is clear that student learning can be measured and actually was being measured in that department on a regular basis. All that had to happen to make this clear was to ask for a copy of the syllabus for the course that covered areas from a particular

Exhibit 4.1   Characteristics of Good Student Learning

SMART: Characteristics of a Well-Defined Student Learning Outcome

A student learning outcome (SLO) focuses on specific behaviors, attitudes, abilities, and other characteristics that a student will demonstrate or possess as a result of instruction or other programmatic activity. It must be SMART:

Specific: SLOs should be specific to a program and stated in clear, definitive terms.

Measurable: SLOs must be stated in terms that are clearly measurable quantitatively or qualitatively. The use of action verbs in SLO statements can maintain a focus on measurability. In addition, programs should consider whether data collection for a particular SLO is reasonable and feasible given program resources.

Attainable: Programs should consider the reality of what they hope to achieve. SLOs should be a reasonable statement of what the program can contribute in terms of student skills, knowledge, and abilities. Know your students and your program!

Results oriented: SLOs should focus on the end result rather than an action to be implemented or provided by the program. They should be clearly stated in terms of what exactly a student should know, be able to do, or value.

Time bound: SLOs should be framed in such a way that they can be measured within a time period over which the program has some control.

Source: Adapted from University of Central Florida (2004).

departmental outcome. Obviously even concepts that are difficult to measure precisely can be used in an assessment plan.

Institutions must provide support for faculty and departments as they develop and revise their mission and outcomes. Since most faculty were never taught how to write an outcome that is measurable, it is important that they be given the proper tools and information so that they can do this well. Nothing is more frustrating to a faculty member who has struggled to create outcomes than to be told that they were not written correctly. In fact, many outcomes written by departments are not measurable and will not result in meaningful and useful information. Faculty need access to workshops and staff members who can help them as they develop disciplinary outcomes. One technique that has worked is to first provide a workshop or a Web-based overview of the basics of writing outcomes. Then it is important to follow this up with specific feedback so that the faculty and department can revise the outcomes.

Faculty work within their disciplines, and many feel that there are differences between their specific learning outcomes and other areas. Although one-on-one conversations between a department and the assessment director may be time-consuming, they nevertheless can provide crucial information to enable the department to create meaningful and measurable outcomes. Asking a department to think of an "ideal graduate" from their program is an excellent way to get faculty thinking about the outcomes that are most important within their specific discipline. Often when faculty begin to think about this "ideal" student, they start to consider the skills, knowledge, behaviors, and beliefs that they want to see in their graduates. Unfortunately, many departmental assessment plans were created by looking at what data they had available rather than thinking about what they really wanted their graduates to gain. Using the "ideal graduate" exercise can help faculty move back to the beginning of the process and focus on what they want to foster in their students so that resulting measures will give them information that can be transformative.

Collaboration, trust, and good communication between the assessment leadership and individual departments are important facets of a campuswide transformative assessment paradigm. If the outcomes that are developed are not meaningful, then no matter how wonderful and exciting the measurement tool, no one will use the data. The outcomes that are developed must focus on the big picture and be important; otherwise, they will lead to bean counting and low levels of faculty involvement. Therefore, ongoing training and individualized feedback are important keys to moving from an accountability assessment process to one that is transformative.

Creating and Identifying Meaningful Direct Measures

Once meaningful and measurable outcomes have been accepted by the department, measures must be developed. Many faculty have experience in measuring their students' learning within the context of a course, but they sometimes have difficulty when looking across a department's curriculum. A faculty member once stated, "We knew a lot more about what our students know before all of this assessment stuff." This statement, probably felt by many, is often accurate. When a faculty member hears a remarkable anecdote or receives an exciting e-mail from a former student, that information is meaningful and valuable. Yet trying to get that same level of richness and detail in a systematic way is extremely difficult. Faculty often feel that measuring outcomes for assessment purposes should be precise and quantitative. Because of this, they may fail to see that they already have rich, meaningful, qualitative information. Most faculty are already using class discussion, papers, exams, or projects to measure student learning within a course, and this material can easily be used as a departmental assessment tool.

Nevertheless, there is nothing wrong with measurements that are precise and quantitative. Many departments use senior capstone exams or licensing exams as measures for specific outcomes. As long as the data gathered are useful to the department, the measure is most likely a good one. Universities have huge amounts of student learning data. In every course, each student demonstrates learning in a wide variety of ways. Faculty need to be able to see how these course-embedded assignments can also be used for assessment.

Providing information about what makes a good-quality measure can be done using campuswide workshops and other means of large-scale dissemination of this information (see Exhibit 4.2). But working individually with departments is an important part of this process. Just as a student's ability to write at higher levels of competency grows by working with a faculty member discussing and rewriting drafts, departments gain skills and confidence in meaningfully measuring learning outcomes by hearing focused and formative evaluations of their assessment plans. The key is to ensure

---

Exhibit 4.2   Characteristics of a Good Measure

Direct Measures of Student Learning

Direct measures of student learning are those designed to directly measure what a student knows or is able to do. They use actual student work products for evaluation. Commonly used direct measures include evaluation of:

- Capstone projects or exams

- Culminating experiences (for example, an internship summary or senior thesis)

- Juried review of student projects or performances

- Student work samples (case study responses, research papers, essay responses)

- Collection of student work samples (portfolios)

- Exit exams (standardized or proprietary exams or locally developed exams)

- Pre- and posttests

- Performance on licensure or certification exams

Continued

Exhibit 4.2 *Continued*

Indirect Measures of Student Learning

Indirect measures of student learning are those that indirectly determine what a student knows or is able to do. Often they focus on how a student perceives her or his own level of learning or satisfaction with some part of her or his education or experience. Some examples of indirect measures include:

- Surveys (of students or alumni, for example)

- Exit interviews

- Employment or graduate school placement rates

- Retention and graduation data

- Demographics of student population

- Focus groups

that these are formative. The feedback must be given in time to rewrite and sometimes to rethink an area or a measurement.

Not only will measurements and their associated outcomes sometimes need to be clarified and rewritten, departments should look at their entire annual assessment process as a formative one that leads into the next year's process. In this way, assessment will continue to evolve, and faculty will become increasingly better at understanding what students know and areas that may need modification. When faculty become accustomed to asking, "What other information would we like to have?" at the end of the assessment cycle, they are primed to modify and enhance their existing assessment plan and make their work ever more transformative.

Developing Surveys and Other Indirect Measures

Even with descriptions of measures that are meaningful, sometimes the information that is gathered is not useful. If survey items are flawed or invalid, the response rate is too low, or the data are lost, the measurement of an outcome becomes useless. Satisfaction or experience surveys may be a tool that departments use, but many faculty do not have the training to help them write high-quality survey items that will gather the information needed.

Every institution should have an assessment or institutional research staff person who can help in the development of survey items. Providing this support can encourage departments and help them see that they are not alone in this process. They have the support of the institution behind them! Faculty who learn survey writing skills will find that they can help in writing exam items. This fact can help faculty bridge the perceived gap between assessment of student learning and the teaching process.

Many institutions already send out surveys to recent graduates and other alumni. Using current technology, it is relatively simple to add a set of survey items that will be seen only by graduates of a particular department. When the institution asks departments for this set of questions, it has to be done only once, and then the data can be collected each year without additional involvement of the faculty (unless, of course, the faculty want to modify items). By adding these types of departmental items to alumni satisfaction surveys, departments can get data they need without having to track, create, and send individual surveys. Clearly this is a situation in which everyone can gain.

Surveys are not the only type of indirect measure that can be used to gain information on student satisfaction and experiences. Other creative and unique methods for gathering data can be used. One example is a tool used by Stephens College. Seniors are asked to write a cover letter for their capstone portfolio that is addressed to the faculty in their program. Within the letter, students must address outcomes that they perceived as met and those not met. More important, students must then describe why those outcomes were met or not met and what the department could have done differently to have provided more support for those outcomes. The results from these subjective and qualitative letters provide a rich and detailed set of information to faculty that clearly can be used to enhance curriculum, pedagogy, and many other areas.

Indirect measures might also include participation rates for guest speakers or research symposia, for example. Asking students to reflect on their own learning can be a powerful, though indirect, measure of how well a department is reaching its goals. These types of student responses are powerful and bring a sense of the personal nature of student learning. But data do not always have to come from the student. There are other methods for learning about how much a student knows.

Departments that require internships have a wonderful tool for assessing, albeit indirectly, what students are demonstrating. Supervisor reports or practicum evaluations can give a great deal of information to a department. Employer surveys can also be an important measure for determining what alumni are able to do after graduation. There is no limit on the type of information that can be useful in measuring departmental outcomes. However, creating and recognizing these opportunities for indirect measures are sometimes difficult to see from within a department. Having staff in institutional support (assessment director, teaching support center staff, for example) who will work with the department to brainstorm new ideas or help identify measures that exist outside the department can make the difference in how well faculty respond to the assessment process.

Faculty Advisory Committees

Without faculty buy-in, transformative assessment processes will never work. But more than just buy-in is needed. Faculty must own the process of measuring student learning outcomes. They have control over the curriculum, and they must also design assessment activities that will give them important information that can be used to modify pedagogy and enhance student learning.

In describing the process of building a meaningful assessment program at Pennsylvania State University, Michael Dooris (1998) said that "the major principles were that assessment at Penn State should be a grassroots program, owned by the faculty who own the programs but centrally coordinated and supported" (p. 5). Faculty are used to creating and updating their own departmental curriculum, but they are not usually involved in looking at learning and assessment at the institutional level.

Faculty are necessary for institutional-level transformative assessment activities to be sustained. Getting the faculty involved at this level can be difficult. Nevertheless, their participation and leadership on institution-wide assessment committees is important for several reasons. First, faculty bring widespread knowledge about the institution to the committee. Many have an excellent sense of institutional history and often know what has been tried before and whether it worked. Of course, this kind of "but we already did that" perception may be difficult to deal with, but a working knowledge of previous attempts can help to guide current decision making.

Second, faculty on an assessment advisory committee will be better at bringing other faculty onboard. Some faculty may be early adopters who buy in quickly and are highly supportive. This is extremely helpful. But it is also important to bring in faculty who may be a harder sell. If the curmudgeonly department chair has been part of the planning process, others will assume correctly that her or his concerns have been addressed and solved. In essence, by providing a place in the communication process for those who might later have derailed the new idea, the new concept is stronger because many issues will have already been incorporated into the process.

A third reason that faculty are important to an institution-wide advisory committee is that they will learn more about the process of assessment and can promote transformative assessment and educate other faculty within their departments. This can help to focus the dialogue on what is known about student learning and how it is measured. By involving faculty in the process of planning for assessment, it is possible for an institution to find that "faculty resistance has been replaced by active dialogue about implementing assessment plans" (St. Ours & Corsello, 1998, p. 6).

Finally, when faculty are involved in the development and implementation of the assessment process, they know why decisions are made and how the process works. In order for assessment to have the potential to change an institution, those who work the most with students academically must have responsibility for the ongoing success of the process. If, as Welsh and Metcalf (2003a, 2003b) indicate, faculty often see institutional effectiveness activities as a threat to the tenure process and academic freedom, faculty leadership is not only important; it is imperative.

Supporting the Use of Assessment Data

Once assessment data are gathered, they must be used. On the surface, this seems a simplistic statement. However, it is amazing how much information exists on college campuses that is never used. There are drawers and files filled with assessment data that are stored on the chance that an accreditor might one day want to see the data—but most never do. After working diligently to collect the data, many faculty are exceedingly disappointed when they learn that no one ever wanted to see this information. However, the purpose of transformative assessment is to gather data that will be useful to departmental decision making, not to an outside accrediting body. So the use of assessment data should be supported within the context of the department or unit.

There is a mind-set that must be shifted in most cases. Many faculty have come to believe that assessment is done only for the purpose of accountability. Therefore, it is for "someone else" to see. The reality should be that the data are for those who gather it. The individual departments and units must create time and methods for analyzing and using the data they collect. They may require support from the institution to do so.

Departments need to be assured that the data they collect will not be used against them. They need to know that it is the use of the data they collect that is more important. Assessment data used for transformation should always be considered formative, never summative. Deans and other decision makers must understand that the assessment process will work only if it is transparent and honest. Departments may be assuming that they must demonstrate that they are meeting all of the outcomes in order to gain resources or other additional funding. If this were the case, then the bar would always be set low and departments would never investigate areas in which they may know that they will fall short. In this kind of situation, the goal is to pretend that everything is working perfectly: students are all learning exactly what the department wishes for them to learn. But this is rarely the case. There should always be a goal to reach for, an outcome that is important and difficult to attain.

Therefore, deans, provosts, and other senior administrators should welcome the department that demonstrates that it is not quite meeting its outcomes (as long as the department has described an action plan that will get students closer to the learning outcomes that are described). Institutional support and appropriate resources should be allocated to departments and units that are willing to show that they are reaching for a high level of achievement. Once this happens with a few departments, others will quickly see that the resources are going to the departments that are using their assessment data to enhance and even transform their pedagogy, curriculum, and student learning.

The office for assessment, along with the provost, should be an advocate for this type of paradigm shift. Often deans have allocated resources based on other mechanisms and have not had the data available that would tie assessment with planning and planning with budgeting. There are several ways to work with the deans and other decision makers to help them realize the value of supporting departmental improvement. One method to help educate and work with deans is to provide easily readable information from departments. If a dean already has a system in place for gathering budget information, it is doubtful that she or he will recognize the need for gathering additional information. However, if that information can be presented to the dean, it may provide enough useful evidence that she or he begins to use this regularly. And when that happens, the institution is closer to the goal of tying assessment, planning, and budgeting together and supporting the use of transformative assessment data. Several assessment management system databases are available and can be used to run reports for deans, department chairs, or other appropriate members of the university community.

The support that is given to individual faculty and departments is important to creating a culture that gathers, analyzes, and, most important, uses student learning data. In addition, once these data have been collected and used for teaching and learning, they can still be used to demonstrate accountability to others.

Professional Development and Support for Scholarly Work

Several elements of the assessment process can result in scholarly work. Knowing what and how much students are learning can lead to interesting research studies that focus on pedagogy, curriculum, or innovations in teaching. For example, knowing that a particular course that involves service-learning engages students and leads to higher levels of learning is important information. This type of research should be encouraged by institutions and departments. Support for faculty who are using assessment data to inform their research is important and can gain larger-scale faculty acceptance of the assessment process.

Departments that have collected data on student learning may begin to see patterns in learning, or they may have developed an innovative measurement for a particular disciplinary outcomes. These should be shared. Often, however, faculty may not see the results of their assessment process as potential publications. They may need someone to point out that the work that they have done has value above and beyond the department decision making. The assessment office may be one of the few places on campus that sees the assessment work done across campus, and this can be an opportunity for that office to encourage the department or a specific faculty member to consider sharing this work. Sometimes the support will be verbal encouragement or even editing work. Sometimes there can be financial support for travel to a professional conference or to help pay for research assistance. The important aspect of this is that faculty and departments can begin to value the work done in assessment as a positive, scholarly approach to disciplinary teaching and learning.

There are many higher education and assessment conferences that are available regionally and nationally. Assisting the travel of a faculty member to one of these as an attendee is also an important form of support for professional development. Faculty who attend a higher education conference that is not disciplinary specific may be amazed at the range of sessions offered and the techniques used at other institutions. They often come back to their home campus as the biggest proponents of the assessment office and the development of meaningful and appropriate processes. As a result of attending a conference on general education and assessment, one faculty member has since led her department in the development of creative measures for learning in economics and the creation of a senior capstone course. Without the financial support of her institution, the faculty member would never have attended this conference.

Sustained Institutional Support

Recognizing that faculty often have legitimate concerns about the assessment process, there are several areas where institutions can focus their efforts to work toward sustaining and developing faculty involvement with teaching, learning, and the assessment of student learning. Katie Brown (2001) has suggested eight areas for institutional commitment to enhance faculty involvement in assessment, summed up by the acronym "$UPPORRT":

- Financial commitment: For any activity to be sustained, there must be financial support and sufficient resources. The assessment process is no different. The institution must provide the necessary funds for ongoing work and changing needs that will occur as needs are identified and areas are addressed.

- Understanding by administration: The senior administration must publicly support the need for assessment and must be able to communicate this to the community, board of trustees, and faculty. In addition, an administration that is supportive of faculty involvement in assessment will regularly read and use the data that result from the assessment process. They will pay close attention to reward structures for faculty working with assessment data.

- Professional development: An institution must provide ongoing professional development focusing on assessment-related skills. On-campus workshops are part of this; so is support for travel to regional and national assessment conferences. "Institutions need to be prepared to support broad-based exposure to assessment for faculty" (Brown, 2001, p. 9).

- Promise: Faculty must believe that the work they do in assessment will never be used against them. The institution must make and hold to the promise that assessment data will be used only to learn about what students know and to inform decision making about curricular and pedagogical issues. A spirit of trust is essential if transformative assessment is going to make a difference.

- Organizational modeling: An institution that has at its heart a culture of assessment is one that will model the use of formative feedback at all levels. "If frontline academic administrators were to open themselves to honest, anonymous feedback from their faculty in ways similar to the way we ask faculty to seek and use student feedback for improvement, we could probably overcome much initial resistance from faculty" (Brown, 2001, p. 10).

- Rewards: A substantive and effective reward structure must be put in place to demonstrate that the institution values faculty involvement with the assessment process.

- Resources for assessment: Although financial resources such as rewards are an important part of demonstrating the significance of faculty work in the assessment area, other resources must be available as well. There must be support staff or faculty with appropriate release time in place to encourage and guide the assessment work across campus. Sufficient technological resources for gathering alumni surveys or databases for storing assessment results must be accessible to all who need them. Resources include the human and technological kind, but no one should ever underestimate the importance of space and location for assessment offices and work space.

- Time: "Institutional transformation does not occur overnight (even if we desperately want it to happen before our next accreditation visit)" (Brown, 2001, p. 10). The development of a meaningful transformative assessment process cannot and should not be rushed. Changing paradigms is a slow process, and if true transformation is going to result, it needs sufficient time and energy. The goal is not an assessment plan that will gain reaccreditation; it is a focus on student learning that allows the data to guide improvement in an ongoing way.

To gain faculty support and leadership in the assessment process, institutional support is vital. Resources focusing on time and money are essential. But it is not only about funding and an occasional course release. Faculty work very hard at what they do, and when their work in assessment goes unnoticed or ignored, they will not continue to be involved with assessment. Recognition of faculty contributions to departmental and institutional assessment work can demonstrate the true collegiality and camaraderie that are hallmarks of effective faculty-administration relationships.

Assessment of student learning, like the curriculum, should be under the ownership of the faculty. Faculty are at the heart of the assessment process because they are, with students, the core of the teaching and learning process. To separate assessment from teaching and learning (as higher education has done for the past two decades) is to believe that assessment of student learning is not part of the educational process.

Transformative assessment is much more than an accountability system. It is how faculty know how much students are learning. Although faculty may not be the authors of a particular alumni survey, they are certainly the most important audience for its results. Institutions would do well to provide resources, support, encouragement, and rewards for faculty as they teach, measure student learning, and study what is working.

5

Transformative Assessment Across Student and Academic Affairs

Higher education is about student learning. Much of the learning that is measured occurs within the classroom and other academic areas. However, because most students spend only twelve to fifteen hours each week in the classroom, they clearly are elsewhere the rest of the time. Some of this time is spent on activities that may not be considered learning (sleeping or socializing, for example). But many cocurricular activities are crucial to the student development process and should be assessed. In addition, many elements within institutional mission statements focus on areas of leadership, citizenship, and global diversity issues. These types of broad goals are often not part of a student's academic major but are intentionally developed within residence life and student affairs areas.

In order for an institution to look across programs and services and assess its effectiveness, an assessment plan must be integrated and at least relatively comprehensive. In addition, many institutional mission statements include items that are not specific to an academic discipline and, indeed, may not be focused on within a specific department. Ethical leadership, for example, is not a topic within most departmental curricular offerings. Commitments to diversity, justice, or the common good are regular parts of institutional mission statements but not always included within academic disciplines as a specific and measurable goal.

Since many of these mission elements are considered important to postsecondary education, they must be assessed and are important enough to assess well. These elements are much more often explicitly stated within student affairs or student life areas within an institution. Therefore, assessment planning must be integrated across the institution, specifically including academic and student affairs.

On many campuses, however, there are often political, theoretical, and other gaps between those who work in academic affairs and those who work in student life. Bridging this divide, which has real barriers, is difficult. But it is essential. George Kuh and Trudy Banta (2000) have identified three obstacles to collaboration between faculty and student affairs staff: cultural-historical, bureaucratic-structural, and institutional leadership.

Cultural-historical impediments to collaboration across campus focus on perceived lack of trust and respect between academic and student affairs. "Suspicion about motives and values is occasionally exacerbated by perceived competition for resources. This competition can lead to a sometimes irrational and almost always dysfunctional territorialism that makes faculty and student affairs staff concentrate on protecting their 'turf' for fear of losing some of what they have" (Kuh & Banta, 2000, p. 6). Schroeder (1999) has identified another type of historical barrier: the seemingly obvious in-class (academic) versus out-of-class (nonacademic) learning experiences. In-class learning is often perceived as more important and more closely tied to the mission of the institution.

Bureaucratic-structural barriers focus on the institutional organization of academic and student affairs. Governance structures in academic affairs are often very different from those in student affairs. Conversations across campus can be difficult when there is no organizational structure to support these collaborations. Even daily time schedules between faculty and student affairs are different. Faculty are usually on campus between 9:00 and 5:00 and rarely come in on weekends or evenings unless they are doing specific research. Student affairs staff, however, often are on call twenty-four hours a day, and because they work regularly with student groups, they often spend hours in the evenings working directly with students. There is also often a salary differential between faculty and student affairs staff. Faculty typically make a higher average salary than those in student affairs. And because value is often tied with income, the work of faculty is often seen as more highly valued by the institution.

The third category of barriers to cross-campus collaboration is that of leadership issues. According to Kuh and Banta (2000), "Many colleagues have told us that key administrators on their campuses do not send a clear message that assessing student learning is a priority; these administrators also fail to articulate the rationale and benefits of collaboration" (p. 7). Administrators usually have not seen role models for productive collaboration between faculty and student affairs, so it is not surprising that many in administration do not see this as meaningful, let alone a priority.

Other institutional barriers can also make collaboration among faculty and student affairs staff difficult. Often faculty view their role as creating knowledge and teaching that knowledge, and they view all other roles as at best secondary. This means that any cocurricular activities that might take student time away from studying and preparing for class is working against the goal of faculty (Zeller, Hinni, & Eison, 1989). Because faculty typically identify with a specific department and discipline first and the institution second, the goals of the larger campus community may not be a priority for them.

Collaboration rather than a lack of communication across campus is much more likely to lead to improvement and enhancement. Moving out of the silo mentality that exists on many campuses is vital to an integrated and transformative assessment process. The difficulty is moving into collaborative systems; institutions of higher education are not known for moving quickly into new and innovative structures. But without significant and meaningful collaboration across campus, knowing the full extent of student learning and experiences will be impossible. In order for change to occur, all institutions need to be willing and able to gather information about students from all areas (Banta & Kuh, 1998). While collaboration can be difficult and time-consuming, the benefits can far outweigh the costs.

The call for collaboration between academic and student affairs is not a new concept. Kelli Smith (2005) indicates that the first published statement of the need for collaboration goes back to 1949 and has been an ongoing plea: "Yet, while this type of collaboration is continually espoused in the student affairs literature, a parallel call for collaboration is absent within the academic affairs literature" (p. 16).

Student Affairs Assessment

While much of the literature on assessment practices in higher education focuses on assessment within an academic department, there is a large category focusing on assessment of student affairs and student life areas. According to M. Lee Upcraft and John Schuh (1996), "Assessment is any effort to gather, analyze, and interpret evidence which describes institutional, divisional, or agency effectiveness" (p. 18). The concept of effectiveness and assessment in student affairs often goes beyond what is usually focused on in academic assessment. It "is not restricted to students, but may include other constituents within the institution such as the faculty, administration, and governing boards, and outside the institution such as graduates, legislators, funding sources, and accreditation agencies" (Schuh, Upcraft, & Associates, 2001, p. 4).

Although the general principles of assessment are the same across the institution, the types of data and the populations from which data are gathered may differ in areas of student affairs. For example, an academic department often assesses the content knowledge of students through a portfolio or an exam. Student affairs assessment processes are typically broader and encompass affective areas (and sometimes physical ones too) in addition to the cognitive domain. Student affairs assessment staff may measure levels of satisfaction with the campus or residence halls for example. These types of measures are extremely important for understanding retention trends on campus, but they are rarely measured within an academic department. In addition, student affairs areas often have several ongoing benchmarks focusing on alcohol awareness, student safe sexual practices, and diversity. The areas for assessment are useful for the institution as a whole, and these data can inform teaching and classroom practices as well.

On one campus, a student survey on cheating behaviors was planned. This initiative came through a student affairs committee, but obviously the findings are of great interest to faculty too. The data have been used to create new pedagogies and course assignments that are less likely to create an atmosphere in which cheating and plagiarism will occur. This information also was important to work that was being done through student affairs on the student honor code.

Integrated and Campuswide Assessment

Trudy Banta and George Kuh (1998) offer suggestions for ensuring that a collaborative, integrated, and campuswide assessment planning process can work. The six themes examined here can help to support an institution that is moving toward gathering effective cross-campus data regarding student learning and experiences.

First, the administration must model a commitment to gathering assessment data and using those data to make good decisions. When both student affairs staff and faculty can see that assessment is valued, rewarded, and used, cooperation is more likely to occur. Banta and Kuh (1998) also suggest that the administration should support faculty-student affairs teams to travel to and present at regional and national conferences focusing on assessment and institutional effectiveness issues.

Second, Banta and Kuh suggest that both faculty and student affairs should have responsibilities for planning curriculum and assessment. Student affairs programming often has at its heart an awareness of the need for ongoing student development work. Entering first-year students often have a dualistic way of viewing theories and decisions (Perry, 1999). For example, incoming students often want to know what the "right" answer is and become frustrated by the often multiple perspectives that are important for understanding information in higher education. This is frustrating in the classroom, but few academic areas have specifically designed curriculum to help move students from a dualistic point of view to one that takes into consideration different ideas and opinions. However, student affairs staff often create curriculum designed to encourage student development in terms of how they gather and use information from other students, authority figures, Web sites, and the media. By being able to measure students' growth in these areas, student affairs staff can collect information about how successful these programs have been. These data are important not only to those in student affairs: this information can, and often should, be used in the development of general education and even disciplinary areas.

Collaboration among those in student affairs and in academic areas can be fruitful and rewarding. Also, issues of multicultural and diversity education are more often directly addressed by those in student affairs. Research by Richard Light (2001) indicates that conversations and educational experiences with students from another ethnicity were important to students' growth, especially that of white students. The students whom Light interviewed explained that collaborative work with other students, especially those from different backgrounds and cultures, helped them make choices that improved what they got out of college. Light states, "A key theme in students' interviews is the strong interplay of different features of campus life. Course choices, advising, and decisions about residential life do not stand in isolation" (p. 3). Students experience their education as much more than a collection of the courses they take. Institutions that wish to use assessment data for transformation need to integrate academic and student affairs in order to see the integration of student life on campus.

Banta and Kuh's third suggestion is about effective collaboration between academic and student affairs staff: "Collaboration between academic and student affairs is more likely when the groups have a common view of what matters in fostering student learning at their institution" (p. 45). A consensual concept of what institutional-level student learning outcomes should be can provide a mutual understanding of priorities and definitions. Individual students do not normally discern a difference between academic and student affairs. Instead they usually focus on their own experiences in which there is a great deal of interaction between what happens in the classroom and what happens elsewhere on campus. Therefore, the work of faculty and student affairs staff should interact on many levels. Knowing that there are agreed-on outcomes and priorities can help to support this interaction and even a shared use of some resources.

Banta and Kuh's fourth suggestion is to regularly reinforce students' learning goals by coordinating learning experiences both inside and outside the classroom. Classroom performance measures of student learning can certainly identify what the student knows, but they cannot determine where the student learned it. Was the learning in class? In a study group created by the professor? In the residence halls? To truly transform a campus learning environment, it is imperative that the institution look at the whole process rather than just the classroom. "Unless these two groups work together, particularly on assessment," write Banta and Kuh (1998), "institutions will be unnecessarily limited in promoting educationally purposeful activities beyond the classroom in such learning-rich settings as student residences, libraries, studios, faculty offices, and places of employment" (p. 46).

As faculty and student affairs staff begin to collaborate, Banta and Kuh identify the fifth issue as the need to work with institution-specific outcomes, processes, and measures. For example, if a particular campus outcome focuses on students' self-report data regarding how much time they spend studying, these data become important regardless of who initially gathered the information. Many institutions have turf battles over who "owns" particular surveys or the resulting data. The truth is that the data are owned and should be used by the institution. In other words, it does not matter who gathered the data. If the data are important to the institution, the results should be shared and used by all. The opportunities for cross-campus partnerships increase dramatically with consensus on institutional-level outcomes and the process for measuring these outcomes.

At one institution, the National Survey of Student Engagement (NSSE) had been administered for several years by the student affairs assessment office. Few in academic affairs, however, knew that this information was available. Then a new director of the institutional teaching center was hired who was not aware that the NSSE data were considered to be "owned" by those in student affairs. After she asked for the information, she was thrilled to discover that those in the student affairs assessment area wanted very much to share the data but did not know how to go about publicizing the results. A happy collaboration began that continues between academic and student affairs on that campus.

The sixth theme that Banta and Kuh (1998) identified is to use assessment data to improve the entire student experience on campus. Often faculty focus on student learning within the specific discipline, but other areas of the student experience are also important to how and what a student might learn. Advising and library hours are two examples. If students are frustrated because the hours of the library do not fit in with their perceived needs, the amount of time spent with study groups or individual research time could be compromised. Working together across campus allows for elements of the student experience that indirectly affect student learning to be identified and discussed. At one private university, students identified issues with access to computer labs during the evening and night hours. Since many faculty were not on campus during these times, this was not something those in academic affairs identified as a problem area. Several surveys hosted by student affairs staff, however, identified computer lab hours as a large issue for students. Once these data were shared with a campuswide committee, changes were made to the computer lab hours, increasing the amount of time that students were able to spend working on individual and group projects that required technology.

Clearly, integrating the assessment work and enhancing the collaboration among those in student affairs and those in faculty affairs can be a positive and necessary step in moving toward a culture of transformative assessment. Magolda (2005), in his study of effective practices in higher education, states:

> One of the many promising practices the research team identified was the integration of students' curricular and co-curricular experiences made possible by collaborations across divisional lines. Student, administrator, and faculty interviewees frequently used the term *collaboration and partnerships* to describe a distinctive campus practice that enhanced the quality of life for students. . . . Collaborative initiatives that favor integrative and holistic approaches to serving students, blurring the boundaries between students' curricular and co-curricular endeavors, are generally functional, newsworthy, and slowly gaining acceptance [pp. 16–17].

This same type of collaboration can also be used to develop learning outcomes. However, Magolda (2005) advises that institutions interested in participating in collaborative initiatives consider the following areas:

- Examine the institutional conventional wisdom. Collaboration in and of itself is not going to enable the institution to become more successful. Magolda advises potential collaborators to focus on integration as a moral undertaking rather than as management strategies in order to build sustainable partnerships that will serve students and the institution well.

- Ensure that the collaboration is meaningful, reciprocal, and responsive. Collaboration simply for the sake of collaboration will not lead to ongoing and sustainable partnerships. The relationship must be based on genuine interest in the data that has mutual benefits.

- Successful partnerships will never be "pseudo-collaborations." Magolda suggests that an ongoing and vibrant collaborative partnership will necessitate that both academic and student affairs have equal weight in decision making and carrying out any proposed changes.

- Successful partnerships will be sustainable when the partners better understand themselves and their academic culture without looking at the collaborating partner as "the other." While members of subcultures of academic and student affairs should agree that they share a mutual goal of "heightening the intellectual climate of the campus," Magolda encourages potential partners to first examine their own culture, including their ideologies, values, beliefs, and other ongoing initiatives that guide current practices and decrease the organizational "cultural divide" (p. 20).

- Successful collaborations respect and expect differences. Collaboration can be difficult. Acknowledging conflict and recognizing that it will occur is important for those who seek to develop healthy, collaborative, and educationally focused partnerships. There must be a culture in place that understands that collaboration will often be time-consuming and will sometimes involve a clash of ideals and expected behaviors.

Collaboration among those involved with transformative assessment across campus can benefit all constituencies, but it can be a difficult shift. Within each institution there are cultures and subcultures that do certain things in certain ways. Overcoming differences and styles can be challenging. But with appropriate and ongoing leadership and faculty-staff agreement on the major issues, this can be a goal worth working toward.

Methods to Integrate Assessment Across Campus

As higher education comes under continued scrutiny and external calls for accountability increase, it becomes more apparent that assessment efforts must be integrated across an institution in order to meet the increased accountability needs. The relatively out-dated notion that faculty are responsible for the intellectual and scholarly aspect of higher education while student affairs areas focus solely on students' social and emotional development must give way to a new paradigm.

Students attend an institution: some may become more involved in student government or fraternity and sorority life, but all are students at the same institution. Student learning takes place in class and outside class, and the complete institution is responsible for developing and measuring learning outcomes that are specific, meaningful, appropriate, and useful. The whole institution is responsible for educating its students. Therefore, collaboration between student and academic affairs is becoming a necessity. The institutional community must work together to provide a "seamless learning environment" (Kuh, 1996). Students work in the classroom with faculty and outside the classroom in labs and research settings; they also work with staff members in the residence halls, with student groups, and in other nonclassroom-based learning experiences. The more that students are involved with learning activities inside and outside the classroom, the more they grow and develop.

How to instill a need and an appropriate process for collaboration may differ from campus to campus. Nevertheless, several elements are essential to successful collaboration. Underlying these is a need for a belief that the assessment process is going to be used to benefit the institution and the student learning process and not to punish individual faculty, staff, or programs. If this basic trust is violated, it becomes difficult for a transformative assessment program to grow and provide data that can be used to truly make a difference.

Communication and Coordination Systems

Most institutions have offices for assessment, institutional research, and other data-gathering units. However, many of these units may have come into existence because of necessity and do not fit into the usual organizational chart. One small private college, for example, does much of its institutional research and data gathering from within the psychology department. The reason is that that is where the faculty member who had the skills and interest in institutional research had her faculty appointment. If this were put into an organizational chart, it would make no logical sense. Why would an institutional-level office be located within a specific academic department? Nevertheless, because of the culture of that institution, this was a process that worked well, but only because of the individuals involved in the situation. This specific faculty member knew and communicated often with the registrar's office, office of admissions, and dean of students. If any of the individuals involved did not share information, this system might fall apart. But the system worked because there was sufficient, regular, and appropriate communication among those who had access to the data.

Other institutions have created their own structure for communication among those involved with assessment data. Whether the communication process is explicitly designed and administered is a crucial point. Regardless of where particular data-using offices are housed, there must be in place a communication process that will work regardless of the individual people involved. Student affairs staff gather a great deal of information about student behavior, developmental changes, judicial issues, and others, yet much of this information is never shared across the campus. There are, of course, some privacy issues that arise with sharing individual student data, but these data in aggregate can inform many aspects of the campus.

Certain questions can be used to determine the levels of communication and coordination among campus units.

- Which offices or units collect data about student learning? Student behavior? Student beliefs?

- How are these offices or units officially connected in terms of reporting structures? If there is no formal reporting structure, what informal communication plans are in place? Are there campuswide committees that involve all of these offices or units? If not, could there be?

- If communication among these offices or units does not occur, who would know? What would happen? How long would it take to recognize that this communication is not taking place?

- Other than the president or chancellor, is there a single university position that has access to the data from these offices or units? If so, does the person in this position regularly analyze these data or read the reports from these offices or units?

- Is there a structure in place for the overall aggregate data to be shared throughout the university community? Are there regularly scheduled times or reports to prompt the sharing of these data?

Overcoming Barriers to Collaboration

Collaboration can be beneficial to the institution, those working with faculty and student affairs, and of course the students, who will benefit from any results of transformative assessment. But there are cultural, historical, and budgetary reasons that often are used as reasons that collaboration would never work. Nevertheless, some methods and trends are available to overcome these barriers.

Intentionally and explicitly discussing the need for collaboration is a good way to start. Although there may be some ways that collaboration between academic and student affairs staff happens "by accident," in most cases it must be overtly planned for. Having support from the institutional leadership in beginning the process is vital. If the leadership supports and recognizes the need for cross-campus data collection and other collaborative efforts, the process becomes smoother. However, on many campuses, the leadership, while not directly opposing collaboration, does not actively support it, and other indirect mechanisms and policies are often in place that discourage collaboration, such as the budgeting process, reporting hierarchies, and even office locations. In these instances, the process will probably begin with those who are working with assessment having discussions and sharing data. As these informal processes and the resulting information are shared, the leadership may begin to view the collaboration as a useful tool. In addition, many of those in academic leadership are often persuaded to work toward collaboration if they see it as a benefit in the accreditation process. Although using the accountability card may help in the short run and get the process moving forward, it should not be the first step. Transformative assessment and collaborative work should occur because it is a good idea, not because it is externally mandated.

Whether the institutional leadership is actively campaigning for collaboration, there are other methods for overcoming barriers to working across campus. An important part of encouraging collaboration is to promote the idea that the educational goals of the institution belong to everyone (Zeller, Hinni, & Eison, 1989). Faculty teach in the classroom, but they spend a great deal of time outside the classroom. When senior administrators explicitly state that education is something for which everyone on campus has responsibility and all play an important role, collaboration may become easier. Advocating for educational goals to be explicitly emphasized across campus is an excellent method for overcoming some of the turf barriers that may exist.

Although all institutions have mission statements, many do not have stated institutional-level outcomes. Creating, discussing, and agreeing on these outcomes leads to the opportunity to have discussions across normal disciplinary and organizational lines. One of the first steps to take in creating institutional outcomes is to form a committee or task force that is small enough to be efficient but has voices from many areas on campus. The committee should be charged by the provost or president to create a draft of institutional-level outcomes that align with the mission statement and are broad-based. Content and knowledge areas are probably already being assessed at the department and program levels, so these institutional-level outcomes should focus on what a graduate from the institution should be able to do, value, believe, or know. At this point in the committee work, creating actual measurements of these outcomes is not important (that will come later). It is crucial to keep the outcomes broad and meaningful. Issues addressed in the mission statement (for example, diversity, ethical leadership, or justice) are the types of outcomes that should be at the forefront of the effort.

Once the committee completes this draft and has approval from the institutional leadership, it should take this draft out to members of the institution—faculty senate, staff assembly, and even student government associations—for their input. Gathering comments and suggestions from across the campus will aid in the efforts toward collaborative assessment work and will allow the whole campus to see what is really important given the specific institutional mission. This process will take time, and it is important to allow for that time. As the committee members share the draft, they should communicate their need for feedback: now is the time to make suggestions, changes, and comments. When feedback is gathered from across campus, the committee can revise the draft and share it again.

This process cannot be done without institutional collaboration. The communication that is necessary for this to work is essential. Ongoing conversations about what a recent graduate should know or do are truly important. When this process works, it will create many occasions for conversation. On one campus, stairwell conversations started up regularly. One of them occurred among a groundskeeper, faculty member, and administrative assistant. They all happened to be in the stairwell at the same time and saw a member of the committee, and they all went to share their thoughts with this person. The resulting conversations created collaboration in areas that no one believed could happen.

The simple concept of informal dialogue can be an important aspect to the eventual success of a collaborative effort toward transformative assessment. Never underestimate the power of a brief chat or office visit. Getting out of the office and walking to another's office can be powerful and make a huge difference. E-mail, telephone conversations, and scheduled meetings are important, but a simple chat that can happen with no advance planning can do more to cement collaborative patterns than many other things. This can break down barriers faster than many administratively led focus groups or mandated lunches. These informal conversations can build the capacity for cross-campus collaboration and strengthened community. By getting to know someone outside a planned meeting, it becomes possible to better appreciate the strengths of that person and the area in which she or he works. For example, the discovery that a student affairs person has experience working with large data sets can be extremely valuable for the institution. Suddenly those skills may be called on by others who would never have asked outside their specific area.

Another way to rise above barriers to collaboration is to discover ways that members of the faculty can work with student affairs offices to augment their courses. One well-known example of this is the use of service-learning. Often service-learning offices are housed in the student affairs areas, and many faculty do not realize that they can be of great use in coordinating work in the community with a specific course. When the collaboration begins in the course level, trust is developed, and the stage is set for ongoing collaboration. And since many service-learning offices assess the work that students do in the community, the faculty member, in conjunction with the service-learning office, may be able to create new methods for measuring specific student learning outcomes. This benefits all areas of a campus, including the students.

Support Systems

Assessment and collaboration are not easy. Both areas are time-consuming and often frustrating, and they may not provide results for some time. Because of this, it is necessary to create support systems to encourage the ongoing work of assessment and collaboration. These support systems can be formal or informal, but in most cases they have the following characteristics:

- They typically have one or two lead facilitators. Although these facilitators may be informal (rather than appointed), typically a single person is the one who will call the group together or to whom others will go when there is an issue that needs to be discussed.

- They meet in an ongoing way. If the support system is formalized by the institution (there is a campus-wide assessment committee), the meetings occur at regular intervals. If the support system is not officially recognized by the institution, meetings still occur at semiregular intervals.

- All present at the meetings are encouraged to participate. In order for a support network or system to function well, the members should feel that they are welcome and that their ideas are important.

- Some amount of complaining always goes on. Although the support system will eventually break down if the meetings become complaint sessions, they often allow for some venting of frustration or discouragement. The support system in place will enable the group to continue to move forward even if there is a roadblock that causes irritation and aggravation.

- There is trust and a feeling of appropriate confidentiality among those in the support system. Members know that they are free to discuss issues and brainstorm new ideas without worrying that what they say will be reported back to a supervisor or coworker.

- Sometimes these support systems also function as a social network, with members going out for lunch or dinner from time to time. These informal relationships can add to the level of trust and make the collaborative process happen more smoothly.

- Members of these support systems or networks often perceive that they are accepted and valued. They believe that the support system is helping them to perform better on their job. The perception typically is that the support system is a positive influence on their performance and their engagement with the institution and the process.

Building Community

Collaborative assessment practices work best when there is a strong sense of community on campus. Obviously data sharing is much easier and more collegial if people know each other. Therefore, building a sense of community will do more than make the institution a more comfortable place to work. It will aid in the data collection and sharing of information and can lead to better communication regarding potential assessment results that can lead to institutional transformation.

Working on joint projects is often a method for building a sense of community. When there is a common, relatively short-term goal, working together can provide the mechanism for getting to know individuals and discovering strengths across campus. It is important that this joint project is something in which there is interest and acceptance, as that will aid in drawing in more people. Several of the regional accreditation organizations are now asking for or have as an option the creation of an institution-specific plan to enhance the quality of education. This type of project has the potential to bring the campus together around common goals and work toward a mutually satisfying conclusion.

As a campus works toward building community it is also important to provide opportunities for informal gatherings. Monthly social events such as a sponsored wine and cheese party can be an opportunity to get to know people from across campus. One campus hosts a lunch each month sponsored by an area or division. They are typically simple gatherings, and those who choose to attend benefit from the networking and communal spirit. These do not always have to be purely social. Larger campus events at the beginning and ending of semesters, for example, are collegial gatherings. A family picnic on campus at the beginning of the semester or even a luncheon to hear from the president can provide the time for informal gatherings that will build community.

In the process of developing collegial relationships, it is necessary to encourage wide participation. If the same people show up time and time again, they may build a wonderful sense of community, but this may not extend to the larger campus community. Inviting and encouraging those who have not yet participated is essential to keep the community growing. Not all will participate, but many more will. And if the leadership of the institution participates, the event will take on added importance.

As part of beginning this community-building process, getting a significant mass of people involved is important. Reaching out to those who already work together and are likely to participate is an excellent way to start. But it is also useful to ask those who might not normally participate to have a lead role. If others see that those usual curmudgeons are participating, they may be more likely to agree to become involved as well. Intentionally asking for others' comments and thoughts and then valuing what others have to say usually leads to the ongoing development of a campus community.

Transformative assessment, as an appropriate, meaningful, sustainable, flexible, and ongoing process, requires a certain level of trust and community in order for the necessary data to be shared so that systematic and consequential change can happen. Change may not be easily done, but it can occur if it is being done for the right reasons and there is collaboration among faculty and student affairs and across the institution. Transformative assessment will be a difficult concept to introduce if there is not some level of collaboration on campus already that, with a little work, can turn into something unique, valuable, and mission specific.

6

Aligning Institutional Mission with Assessment

Elements of a Meaningful Institutional Effectiveness Program

Reading any of the vast amount of literature on assessment and accreditation immediately demonstrates the wide variety of definitions for specific terms, many of which are often used interchangeably. To get any discussion started on the wrong foot, ask a group of educators to differentiate a goal, an outcome, and an objective. Or ask about the definition differences of assessment, measurement, and evaluation.

Unfortunately, higher education often gets bogged down in definitions rather than working with a process that really cannot be specifically defined. As Peter Ewell has often said, "Why do we insist on measuring it with a micrometer when we mark it with chalk and cut it with an axe?" (cited by Southern Illinois University–Edwardsville, 2008). More important than precise definitions of terms is the ongoing knowledge that the assessment process is not an end product but the means to an end: enhanced student learning. The assessment process can demonstrate to others that the institution is doing what it says it is doing (accountability), but the resulting data can also become a catalyst for increasing the quality of teaching and learning, and that can be transformational.

Ewell (1999) has stated that in order for assessment to be authentic, creative, and focused on action, significant areas must be in place: "(a) Taken from the proper value perspective, assessment constitutes a powerful tool for collective improvement that is highly consistent with core academic values and (b) infusion of the logic of assessment directly into classroom and curricular settings is perhaps the most powerful means we have at our disposal to transform the logic of pedagogy itself—from one-way instruction to collaboration and partnership" (p. 147). Assessment can therefore be transformative when it is used to directly inform and have an impact on teaching and learning at the classroom level.

As this chapter begins to look at institutional levels of effectiveness, it can never be forgotten that the whole point of higher education is to educate the student. The singular *student* is used intentionally here. Typically a student comes to a specific institution in order to get a degree, but that degree means something specific. That student has met the standards set by the institution, and they include passing a certain number of specified courses. These courses contain the information that this student should have gained in attaining the degree.

Institutional effectiveness is measured by the progress of students toward reaching the standards set by the institution. It focuses not on what is taught and how, but on what and how much students have learned. So although institutional effectiveness is considered a macrolevel look at institutional-level goals regarding (among other things) student learning, measures of effectiveness are almost always built on the individual student's knowledge and skills gained throughout her or his time at the institution. "The most important element of institutional effectiveness is the impact the institution has on the knowledge base of its students" (Sullivan & Wilds, 2001, p. 4).

In general, institutional effectiveness is considered to be a formal, ongoing, and systematic process that measures quality to ensure the institution and others that the performance level matches the stated purpose of the institution. This usually involves several areas, including assessment, program reviews, strategic planning, and often benchmarking (Welsh & Metcalf, 2003b). Institutional effectiveness uses three main categories of activities in its evaluation: data collection, data analysis, and the use of that resulting information to lead to improvement.

The use of the phrase *institutional effectiveness* as it relates to assessment, accreditation, and higher education was first used in December 1984 when the Commission on Colleges of the Southern Association of Colleges and Schools (SACS) approved an accreditation standard on assessment. James Rogers describes the event by stating that "so controversial and even intimidating was the 'A word' that new terminology had to be found to give a broader and more acceptable definition of the concept. That new term was institutional effectiveness" (1997, p. 1). No longer was it acceptable to merely count the books in the library or show how much money was in the budget (not that it was actually that simple). The standard of institutional effectiveness changed the way accreditation looked at an institution, and this began to change the ways in which an institution looked at itself.

Currently all regional accreditation organizations require assessment of the entire institution and want to see how the institution demonstrates that it is achieving what it says it is. The Middle States Commission on Higher Education, for example, requires that every institution identify the methods used to determine institutional effectiveness. Each of its standards has an assessment element. The commission states that "assessment processes help to ensure that:

- Institutional and program-level goals are clear to the public, students, faculty, and staff.
- Institutional programs and resources are organized and coordinated to achieve institutional and program-level goals.
- The institution is indeed achieving its mission and goals.

- The institution is using assessment results to improve student learning and otherwise advance the institution [Middle States Commission on Higher Education, 2005, p. 4].

Elements of an Institutional Effectiveness Plan

An institutional effectiveness plan should provide the institution with enough information to make effective decisions. In addition, this plan should enable the institution to clarify future directions and establish meaningful priorities. When these are based on the data collected and analyzed, the resulting decisions are more likely to be successful because they will be grounded on the facts and other information available. When data collection and analysis is done in a transparent way, building participation and sharing the decision making, the entire institution has focus and purpose. This can create transformation by improving overall organizational performance based on the realities of student demographics and the changing environmental and educational landscape. When an institution is collaboratively focused on a common purpose and ongoing assessment practices and organizational functioning is geared toward a set of specific and agreed-on goals, the overall efficacy of the institution will increase.

Several important areas are necessary in order to have a meaningful, shared, and ongoing institutional effectiveness plan. Although these may be established in different ways depending on institutional size and culture, the basic elements are necessary for developing the institutional effectiveness process.

Aligning Mission and Goals

An institution's mission statement is the foundation of the development of the planning and effectiveness process. Mission statements sometimes are modified, but rarely are they changed dramatically. The mission tells students, faculty, staff, and the rest of the community what the institution believes in and works toward.

Most mission statements contain what educational psychologists often call "word magic." What this means is that the words all sound great and most people would agree that the mission statement is important and good, but most cannot describe exactly what the mission statement means. The concepts of, say, "global citizenship," "ethical leadership," and the "commitment to the common good" all sound significant and substantial, but few people on any given campus could agree on exactly what these terms mean.

Because mission statements are so difficult to operationalize, it is important that goals of the institution are agreed on. These goals must align with the mission statement but be a behavioral reflection of the mission statement. For example, an institution might have as a set of goals that students will become "lifelong learners" or "responsible participants in their community." These goals are not necessarily measurable, yet they help to define more clearly what the institution might mean by its relatively amorphous but beautifully stated declaration of mission.

Sometimes institutions call their goals "core values" or give them some other label. These are all useful in better describing what is meant in the actual mission statement. For example, North Carolina Central University (NCCU) has this as part of its mission statement: "The mission of the university is to prepare students academically and professionally to become leaders prepared to advance the consciousness of social responsibility in a diverse, global society. The university will serve its traditional clientele of African American students; it will also expand its commitment to meet the educational needs of a student body that is diverse in race and other socioeconomic attributes."

Many of the elements in this mission statement are more clearly identified by the NCCU set of Core Values:

- Excellence in Teaching, Research, Scholarship, and Creativity
- Access to Education and Effective Development Opportunities

- Promotion of Citizenship, Service, and Social Justice
- Appreciation of and Respect for Diverse Perspectives
- Superb Customer Service
- Commitment to Life-Long Learning

As the institution has worked to establish these goals, the elements of the mission statement are reflected in the language chosen. Given this set of core values, it is expected that any departmental or program outcomes will also reflect these ideals.

Clearly institutional goals or core values must align with the mission statement. Elements in the mission should be reflected in at least one area of the developed goals. This process begins the alignment of mission with all activities on campus. Since faculty and staff will use the goals as they develop institutional, departmental, and program outcomes, the stated goals must reflect all areas of the mission statement.

Institutional-Level Outcomes

Outcomes at the institutional level allow the institution to better understand and more fully measure the behaviors, skills, values, and beliefs that graduates of their programs should be able to demonstrate. Assuming that there is alignment from the mission statement, goals, and institutional outcomes, assessing these outcomes measures the degree to which the institution is accomplishing its mission. This is important for several reasons. The first is that the mission statement identifies publicly what the institution is doing. If no assessment is ever done at the institutional level, there is no way of knowing if the institution is actually doing what it has promised. Second, the elements within the mission statement, goals, and institutional outcomes are typically broader than those within an academic department or program. With these broader outcomes (for example, "leadership" or "engaged citizenship"), meaningful measurement will require collaborative work across the institution using both academic and student affairs staff. Finally, institutional-level reflection on the assessment of these broad outcomes can help all areas keep focused on the overall institutional effectiveness plan and process.

As these institutional-level outcomes are developed or redefined, there is a need for widespread cross-campus participation and a sense of openness and transparency in the process. Decisions regarding how particular terms are defined or included can have long-lasting impact. This process can take time, but collaboration and cooperation will help to ensure that the resulting outcomes will be used effectively and implemented widely.

Departmental-, Program-, and Unit-Level Outcomes

Aligning departmental, program, and unit outcomes with the institutional mission statement makes a great deal of organizational sense. However, most academic departments do not look first to the institution as they create learning outcomes for their students. Rather, they look to the content and theories of their professional and academic field, and this is especially true for areas that have specialized accreditation standards that must be met. So instead of looking to align student learning outcomes with the mission statement and the institutional-level outcomes, faculty align with expected knowledge and content from their discipline.

At first glance, this may seem to be a problem. But because the goal of transformative assessment is for those who will use the resulting analysis of data to create the outcomes that guide the measurements, this potential lack of alignment is not typically problematic. Academic departments and programs must have specific outcomes that differentiate themselves from other similar areas. Social work, for example, may be similar in some ways to psychology, but there are sufficiently crucial differences between them that they are different fields with different content, histories, and theories. It would be a huge mistake for an institution to ask academic departments and programs to create similar outcomes.

It is at this point that the institutional core values and goals become important. The core values for The Ohio State University state that the university will:

- Pursue knowledge for its own sake.
- Ignite in our students a lifelong love of learning.
- Produce discoveries that make the world a better place.
- Celebrate and learn from our diversity.
- Open the world to our students.

Given these, it becomes a relatively intuitive process to add new discipline-specific outcomes or modify existing ones that take into consideration areas such as diversity, lifelong love of learning, or engaging students with content and knowledge.

When an institution is moving to a more transformative approach in assessment, asking departments, programs, and units to change what they are doing and line up with institutional dogma is almost sure to lead to impassioned cries for academic freedom—and appropriately so. One of the major tenets of transformative assessment is that the outcomes must be created by those who will use the resulting data. To impose an institutional structure on a department is almost always doomed to failure. Instead, work with the departments to have them create the ways that their specific and important content can be a means to work with students in these goal or core values areas. Recognizing the need for departmental faculty to take the lead, the director of assessment should continue to support and ask questions, but not demand that certain outcomes be added. The outcomes are the creation of the department or unit and should be modified only by those within the program.

As might be imagined, relying on so many across campus to create outcomes and align some of them with institutional values may take some time. But it is much better to take additional time during the creation of the outcomes than to try to fix them after they have been put into place. At one institution, department, unit, and program outcomes were created about eighteen months before the regional reaccreditation visit was to take place. Not surprisingly, these outcomes were created in a vacuum, and they were based on currently available data. Faculty looked to see what tests or surveys had high numbers of student respondents, and they used that measure to produce the outcome. This, of course, is a backward system and is not going to generate data that will likely be transformative. Although this system resulted in many assessment plans and a great deal of data, most were not used in any effective way. The regional accreditor was not fooled: the institution was cited for not having an integrated assessment plan or process. In addition, in the following years, many departments had a hard time thinking of assessment in any other way. It has taken several years for faculty at this institution to begin seeing assessment as an ongoing and potentially useful process.

The lesson to be learned is that it is much better to allow the time needed for faculty and staff working within departments and units to produce meaningful and high-quality outcomes that can be integrated with the overall institutional effectiveness plan.

Appropriate Measures

Colleges and universities are overflowing with data. There are fact books containing years of demographics, student portfolios filled with writing products and projects, and huge amounts of information kept on student behavior in the residence halls, library use, and retention information. Why, then, is finding appropriate measures an issue at all? The problem is that most of the data that exist on college campuses were collected for reasons that have nothing to do with assessing student learning. In fact, those data could be used for that reason in many cases. The key is to begin with the outcomes.

If departmental, unit, or even institutional outcomes have already been approved, finding appropriate measures may be as simple as matching existing data sets with an outcome. For example, if a departmental outcome focuses on specific skills that graduates of a kinesiology program need, one appropriate measure would be the passing rate of students on their certification exam. Linking the information that is already being tracked with meaningful outcomes is an easy and important way to gather the information that is necessary for the program. In the case of departments that do not have certification exams or licensing requirements, data may already be available in the form of student work products that are embedded in existing course work. These papers, exams, and projects can easily be used to demonstrate an individual student's knowledge to be used for the course instructor to assign a grade and to be gathered across the department to look overall at students' knowledge in that particular category. Faculty are already using these to measure student learning at the individual level, so it is relatively simple to use them for departmental assessment too.

Sometimes an outcome may not seem to be linked with any existing data. In this case, the appropriate measure may take a bit more creativity to develop. For example, one outcome for a general education program focusing on global awareness states, "Students will demonstrate the ability to develop informed judgments about global issues." In this case there may not be any existing data that could be used to measure this. Asking, "What do we need to see in order to know that a student has done this?" may be a good way to focus on the appropriate measure. Clearly student work done that focused on a global issue and required the student to make a judgment and back it up with research, literature, or discipline-specific experiences could show how many students had met the outcome. At one institution, faculty who taught courses in this general education area met regularly to determine how to collect information on this outcome. There are many ways that this could be done: a new assignment for a project could be created that could be slightly modified for each specific course within this general education category; all students taking a course within that category could respond to the same writing prompt in a final exam; even interviews could be done with seniors after they had taken their general education sequence asking specifically for an example of an informed judgment about a current global issue. The point is that there is no one correct measure. Many could be used, and having multiple measures could provide even broader information.

At the institutional level, creating appropriate measures that align with the campus-wide outcomes can require even more creativity. These outcomes are often more difficult because they are broad and may involve areas that are rich, complex, and hard to measure. Critical thinking, understanding global justice, and leadership are some of the areas that are not easily measured. The tendency, then, is not to list these areas as institutional-level outcomes. This is the same mistake that has been made for decades and has caused assessment to be seen as bureaucratic bean counting rather than as a method to gather necessary information with the potential to transform an institution and higher education in general.

It is especially important to create multiple measures for these hard-to-measure areas. Any one measure will not address the issue sufficiently, but several may give enough information that the institution can use to triangulate. In other words, several measures will get a lot closer to understanding these concepts than a single measure can. Taking a single one from the examples above, leadership can demonstrate the difficulty of the process but also the potential gold mine of information that can be used for institutional effectiveness.

The first step is to determine what definitions of the elements in the outcome are specific to the institution. This can be a time-consuming process if there is no agreed-on set of terminology, but time spent here will most certainly be saved later. Campuswide discussions, focus groups with representative samples of institutional constituents, and reviewing the literature are good ways to begin the process. The Council for the Advancement of Standards in

Higher Education (CAS, 2007) has created several broad outcomes and examples of how these outcomes might be measured.

In the CAS standards, "Leadership Development" is defined in this way: "Articulates leadership philosophy or style; Serves in a leadership position in a student organization; Comprehends the dynamics of a group; Exhibits democratic principles as a leader; Exhibits ability to visualize a group purpose and desired outcome." Sharing this list with campus constituents may be one way to suggest possible appropriate measures. An institution with the desired outcome of leadership could begin to measure several of these specifically. Students could be asked on an exam to state a coherent leadership philosophy and describe specific examples of how they had demonstrated this style. Counts could be taken of the number of students who had leadership positions on campus, or a "leadership" transcript could be developed by the institution that listed all organizations that a student had membership in and which leadership positions had been held. In addition, a course of leadership theories could be created, and students could be asked to complete a project in which they identify leadership character-istics. All of this information could provide the institution with evidence regarding students and leadership development.

Some institutions might want to take this even further and look at possible increases in leadership skills over time. What is the student's proclaimed leadership philosophy at the time of her or his first-year orientation? Does that philosophy change by the time these students are seniors? Has a particular student held more leadership positions in college than she or he did in high school? All of these data points are not necessary, but many of them gath-ered together will give a better picture of leadership development than any one of them. It also becomes clear that both direct and indirect measures can be used to measure complex outcomes. Although the definitive answer may never be found, the institu-tion can get closer to an accurate representation of how much stu-dents are learning.

Collaborative and Cross-Campus Analysis of Data

In the example of leadership development, some of the information suggested for measures could come from academic classrooms, and some of it might come from information held within student affairs. Collaboration across the campus in both the creation of institutional-level learning outcomes and the measurement of these outcomes is essential. As described more fully in Chapter Five, collaboration across the institution can be difficult, but it is absolutely necessary in order for a transformative assessment process to lead to ever-increasing institutional effectiveness. Senior-level administrative support and modeling of cross-campus collaboration is vital to its success.

Using the Data to Effect Transformative Improvement

Another essential component of a strong institutional effectiveness process is that the data collected are used. Although this may sound like such an obvious statement, in fact, too much information that has been collected across institutions has never been used. When one director of assessment moved into a new position, she had her staff remove twenty-seven boxes of binders that had been sitting on bookshelves for over six years. Not one binder with its careful color-coding had been opened since the information had been placed into it. The data were never used at the institutional level.

When this happens, it is easy to see why institutional assessment efforts are often viewed as a waste of time, effort, and resources. When data are collected but not used, faculty and staff trust in the administration suffers, and few participants are likely to take part in future assessment efforts. "Faculty tend to have more trust in the academic culture than in the administrative hierarchy" (Welsh & Metcalf, 2003a, p. 447). And faculty resistance is often seen as the most significant reason for failure to fully implement assessment and institutional effectiveness activities (Nichols, 1995; Kramer, 2006).

Improved technology can help with the process of using assessment data more effectively. Databases are now often used to store outcomes, measures, and findings. Once this information is in the database, it can be searched, sorted, and pulled together in a variety of ways. For example, if a department-level outcome is also linked to an institutional outcome, the same data and findings that were analyzed by the department can be integrated with other findings at the institutional level. Although this can certainly be done without database support, the technology can make the process work more smoothly.

Planning and Budgeting

The results of assessment must be linked to the budgeting process. Planning and budgeting—in that order—are essential. Obviously the budget process is crucial to the ongoing existence of the institution. But how the institution chooses to use its resources should be informed by where the resources are needed. And determining where resources are needed can be highlighted by the results of assessment.

One method of incorporating planning and assessment with the budget process is to ensure that strategic planning, quality enhancement, and the institution's budgeting are all part of the cycle (Figure 6.1). In this way, the importance placed on assessment outcomes can lead to continuous improvement, with data used in the decision-making process. Ann Dodd (2004) has seen that accreditation can often be used as a catalyst to move institutions toward this integrated process. She states that "many institutional planners and researchers emphasize the importance of relating planning and assessment initiatives in a continuous cycle to enhance institutional effectiveness. A few add improvement to the planning and assessment cycle in order to strengthen efforts toward institutional effectiveness" (p. 15). An institution cannot function without sufficient and appropriate budgeting. No matter how exciting an academic program is, the institution will

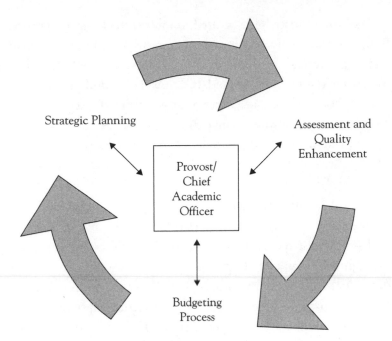

Figure 6.1.   Institutional Planning Diagram

not last if there is not enough money to pay the light bill. But knowing that resources could be used for a variety of academic and institutional programming requires having accurate data on which of these potential programs aligns with the mission of the institution and can be successful.

One of the realities of higher education is that there is a finite budget. Because of this, many institutions use the process of resource allocation and reallocation to ensure that the funding and other resources are going to programs that can best use them. If transformation is going to occur, it will most likely take additional resources, and these resources must come from somewhere. Given this, it seems that the time of the entitled budget may be ending. Institutions must be free to move resources from one area to another so that the most can be done with the available funds and resources.

Assessment data must be used to inform the budgeting process. Innovative and entrepreneurial programs that support the mission and may increase student success in meeting departmental and institutional outcomes should be considered and funded when possible. But just because a program was funded once should not mean that it will always receive funding if, over time, it is not supporting the mission and outcomes of the institution.

Overcoming Resistance

Successful institutional effectiveness programs have found a way to overcome the typical initial opposition that often occurs. As Barbara Wright has said, "The way to a faculty member's head is through the discipline" (2005, p. 1). There are departmental and individual benefits to the process. The assessment process is typically presented in a generic form, with little emphasis on disciplinary differences. "I've always suspected," said Wright, "that the assessment message would get through more readily if faculty were approached through their disciplines" (p. 1). Truly there are many advantages for departments when they begin to embrace (or at least participate in) the assessment process.

One of the first things that departments notice when they begin to use their assessment data is that they are usually doing a pretty good job of educating students. This relatively objective information can mean a great deal to those who have dedicated their lives to their discipline. While most faculty get an occasional thank-you e-mail from a former students, it is especially meaningful to find out the same information from a much larger percentage of alumni. In the same way, for a faculty member teaching an introductory course, finding out that students actually do remember and use the information that was taught can be extremely rewarding.

Another benefit for departments is that the student learning data that they receive is designed to be used to improve the departmental offerings. This can provide information about course sequencing, curriculum, departmental advising, and teaching. As some departments begin to look at the results of their assessment data, they can see more clearly the potential for their students. Many department chairs have approached the assessment process as another mandated, administrative irritation but have found that it provides systematic data that support anecdotal information. For example, an economics department found that students who changed majors from particular areas on campus were less prepared in terms of their quantitative skills. As a result, the department creates a course for students who needed additional math. This modification was successful: the result was better-prepared students in upper-level courses.

Going through the assessment process at the departmental level means that faculty must look beyond the specific courses that they teach and look at the major as a whole. Courses are taken in a vacuum. They should provide an integrated path for students to become experts at an appropriate level within the discipline. Faculty often do not take the opportunity to consider with colleagues how the courses, while taught individually, are part of the whole program. Prerequisite courses lead to advanced courses and the skills and knowledge learned at one level should be used and enhanced at subsequent levels. Departments can use this process to establish better communication among faculty in terms of student expectations and even assignments.

In one psychology department, a faculty member teaching a research methods course found that students did not come with the prerequisite statistics knowledge even though they had taken the course. After talking with the prerequisite course instructor, she discovered, based on test scores in the statistics class, that the students had in fact been taught and had learned the information. After discussion, the instructors decided that one way to help students transfer the content from the statistics course to the research methods course was to use some of the same case studies and examples in both courses. The prerequisite course instructor previewed how that information would be used in the research design course, and the research design instructor then began the course with a refresher on what they had already learned. This information made the students in the department much better prepared for all subsequent courses that used statistical or research skills.

Finally, faculty and staff who might be resistant to the creation and use of an institutional effectiveness plan may begin to understand how useful it can be when they see their departmental- and unit-level outcomes and data as an important part of the institutional educational plan. Students choose to come to an institution in part because of their desired major but also because of the overall institution. Faculty and staff work in individual departments and units, but they too are part of the overall institution, and the work they do with students is important to the university. An institutional assessment plan can help to connect the separate areas across campus without diluting the importance of the individual disciplinary differences.

Providing Adequate Support

Creating, implementing, and using the institutional effectiveness process to transform an institution requires adequate institutional support. Regardless of whether the senior administration has become interested in this process because of external accreditation mandates or because it is a way to know how well the institution is doing, this process will take ongoing resources.

The first of these resources is time. Establishing and then integrating an institutional effectiveness process can be time intensive, and much of that time is required at the planning stages. It may be necessary for other less important activities to be temporarily suspended. Faculty who are involved may need release time, and staff involved may need to have others take over some of their normal duties. There is also a need to begin the process with more time allotted to it than may be considered necessary. This process almost always takes longer than anyone thought it would.

If the initial purpose of implementing an institutional effectiveness plan is for a reaccreditation visit, beginning this process a couple of years prior will probably not give enough time to gather sufficient support and make the necessary cross-campus connections. Whenever possible, the institution should give itself at least five years for full discussion, debate, and decision making. Although some institutions may not take this long, it is much better to have more rather than less time built into the process. One of the worst things that could happen is that a decision is rushed, which could lead to the perception of something being "rammed down the throat" of the faculty.

Another necessary resource is technical support. Most faculty and staff initially do not know how to create formal assessment processes at the departmental and institutional levels. In addition, there may be a need for support in creating and putting up online surveys or other Web-based data collection sites. Statistical support may be needed as well. Wherever the support staff are located should be in a centralized location. One particular office should be able to know what is happening across campus: what measures are used, the type of data that are collected, and how the findings are being analyzed. The assessment or institutional research office may be the place for this support. Many institutions are creating offices or centers for institutional effectiveness as a way to gather information that may be created and initially used at the department or program level but can also be used at the institutional level.

Along with a centralized technical assistance location, there is a need for coordination. While many of the assessment efforts can and should occur in a decentralized way, being able to coordinate the many institutional effectiveness elements is essential. Data from surveys of graduating seniors and alumni, for example, can benefit individual departments. The difficulty is often in getting the information from one place to another. Having a coordinated effort can help to support the campuswide collaboration and use of data. So although not every department wants to analyze the database of results that comes from the National Survey of Student Engagement, for example, most do want to get the information that results of the survey. Planned coordination is an important step in making sure that an institutional effectiveness plan will work in the ways that it was intended.

Another important area to identify because it can support the activities regarding institutional effectiveness is faculty and staff professional development. Institutional effectiveness has at its heart issues relating to student learning and development. Not only can these provide opportunities for scholarship and publication, but these activities can also identify areas that may need improvement. For example, if an institution discovers that students are not as academically engaged as desired, an action plan might be developed to offer more active learning strategies in the classroom. As a result, faculty might take advantage of faculty development workshops that help them to modify their pedagogy.

On one campus, institutional-level assessment activities indicated that students were not maintaining their initially high writing skills. This situation prompted an in-depth look at the existing writing-across-the-curriculum program, followed by a decision for more faculty to incorporate additional writing assignments in many of the courses across campus. Faculty did this and incorporated writing into each of the senior capstone courses. Measures of student writing skills showed increases, and faculty satisfaction increased because they felt that they were better responding to student writing and that this caused students to be better prepared for class because they were doing more writing in individual disciplines.

Creating a Climate for Institutional Effectiveness

An atmosphere that is open to reflection and ongoing learning and improvement should be a hallmark of effective higher education institutions. A campus that uses the results of student learning assessment to inform important decisions will be much more likely to be looking to always improve the student experience. Using these results in a transparent, ethical, and responsible way will be a model for others and will increase the likelihood that all members of the institution will trust the institutional decision-making process. Institutions should also recognize and reward efforts that are made to improve, even if the effort was not at first successful. By encouraging thoughtful educational risk taking, faculty and staff will be able to keep up with the increasingly difficult task of educating the next generation.

By incorporating the elements outlined in this chapter and engaging as much of the campus community in the development and implementation of the process, a cycle of continuous quality enhancement can transform an institution. The development of a common vision and goals will create a climate that is more likely to be focused on student learning and the purposes of higher education. Although the specific needs of students will change over time, an institution that practices ongoing institutional effectiveness will be poised to take on the challenges of the future.

Institutional Implementation of Transformative Assessment

Implementing any type of assessment program can be challenging and frustrating—and ultimately rewarding. But in the process there are many models of implementation and several potential pitfalls that can have an impact on the time spent and the actual outcomes. It is clear that assessment in higher education has many conflicting and sometimes even contradictory purposes. Phillip Kramer (2006) states that "legislators, professors, students, parents, employers and others may be in agreement about some assessment goals (e.g., increasing student knowledge; demonstrating student acquisition of knowledge) but in disagreement about other assessment goals (e.g., use of standardized, norm-referenced assessment instruments, determining responsibility for teaching and learning)" (p. 598).

The process of implementing a transformative assessment plan can bring about stress and anxiety on campus. Trudy Banta and Associates (1993) state that there are apparent and often understandable tensions when discussing assessment because some want to focus on assessment for accountability and others may concentrate on the desire for assessment results important to student learning. There is a problem with focusing on assessment in this way, however. Assessment does not have to be *only* for accountability or *only* for improvement. Transformative assessment can provide both because these are two sides to the same coin. The same type of tension often exists between faculty and administration over issues relating to student satisfaction. Administrators are typically the ones who are getting phone calls from worried or irate parents or unhappy students. The issues may be related to food quality or sufficient parking, but they are calls that few administrators like to get. When the dissatisfaction relates to an instructor or a course, there can be tension between wanting the student (and parents) to be happy with the knowledge that student learning is more important than happiness or satisfaction. However, this does not mean that an instructor cannot have both: satisfied students *and* a rigorous course that pushes students to grow intellectually. Assessment can also meet both accountability and learning enhancement.

Transformative assessment should focus on student learning. The creation of meaningful and measurable outcomes along with appropriate measures can provide the information that informs all decisions about student learning: pedagogy, curriculum sequencing, student preparation needs and admission criteria, resource allocation, and course assignments. When the process is documented, especially focusing on the modifications made as a result of the data analysis, information will be available for accountability to external constituents.

Models of Implementation

Implementing transformative assessment on an individual campus takes time. Different institutions are often at different places when it comes to working with assessment and measures of student learning. Some already have a cadre of interested and motivated faculty working to better understand and use information about student learning; at others, this is not the case. Some institutions have a great deal of senior-level administrative support for the use of transformative assessment, and some are only looking toward the next accreditation visit. The following models represent several approaches to implementing a transformative assessment plan on a campus.

Departmental-Focused Model

Many institutions already have assessment plans in place at the department level. The faculty-focused model of implementation begins with the assumption that assessment of some type has been discussed and worked with on that campus. Often the departmental assessment plans in place are not aligned with the mission of the institution, however. In fact, many are not even aligned with their own departmental mission statement. Unfortunately, as accreditation visits loomed, many departments were told that they had to have an assessment plan, and soon! The problem was that there was usually not a lot of planning about what the outcomes should be and how to ensure that they were meaningful.

In the same way, measures have often been chosen based on data the department already had handy; sometimes the measures are not even aligned with the outcome that they purportedly measured. However, even campuses where not a lot of meaningful assessment is occurring often have a working knowledge about the concept of assessment and an acknowledgment that assessment is a process necessary for accountability.

To begin to move from an accountability perspective to a transformative assessment model, an institution should begin with what is already in place—even if what is in place is not going to work well. Since there can be a lot of negative feelings toward the assessment process, one of the worst things that an institution can do is to go back to the faculty and ask them to start all over again. Even if the assessment process is not working well at the departmental level, time and effort have been put into the plan, and most likely, a lot of time and effort have also been put into talking about and complaining about the process. To many faculty, assessment is just another fad that will soon go away. To ask them to drop what they have already worked on and do something "new" will probably cause them to think that this next "new" assessment will soon be changed also. The reality, of course, is that what is being asked of them is not that new. Rather, it is a substantial modification of the outcomes and measures, but not a change in the overall assessment process.

Phase 1 of the implementation of transformative assessment should start where the departments are: not asking them to start over but to look at the overall picture. Often the way to do this is to work with a single department at a time, with a university assessment person from outside the department asking questions and listening to what faculty have to say. Using the concept of the ideal graduate is an effective way to start (this is discussed more fully in Chapter Four). When faculty within a department are focused on what they want students to learn, they begin to talk about the skills, content knowledge, beliefs, and experiences that they hope a student will have had by the time of graduation. A skillful listener can take this information and work it into several outcomes. Faculty are not usually trained in writing outcome statements, and when they try to do it according to specific outcome rules, they can become frustrated. However, when they talk about wanting their students to, say, "think and write like a historian," they can zero in on what they really want their students to be able to do.

Much of the faculty frustration about assessment comes from the difficulties in trying to find a single set of outcomes that makes sense to the entire department. And because there are often many subdisciplines within a department, trying to settle on "the most important" is almost always bound to bring up old theoretical arguments that will never be resolved. Keeping the focus on the ideal graduate is one way to help the faculty within a department begin to discuss what they want to see in their students.

In the discussions of these broad outcomes, finding some agreement, even if it is the lowest common denominator, can be a start. In one psychology department, the faculty could agree after a three-hour meeting only that students should write in the American Psychological Association style. But once they could agree on that, they began talking more broadly about their mission and goals. Eventually this department had ten meaningful and very important outcomes.

Giving this first phase of the implementation sufficient time is crucial. It may take departments several meetings over multiple semesters to craft their outcomes, and they may have to unlearn some bad assessment habits. It may take awhile for faculty to trust that the assessment plan must be created and designed for their specific department. They might be able to use some of the objectives that they already are using, but it is best not to mention those until they have completely discussed their ideal graduate and developed a description of what they hope to see. At that point, bringing out the outcomes that already exist may allow them to look at these with new perspective. Some of these existing outcomes might fit in well with what they have discussed, others might be replaced, and still others might be tabled for a time. The goal of this first phase is to end up with a few (maybe three to ten) outcomes that elicit general agreement about their importance to the department.

Once the outcomes have been established, the second phase is to ask, "How do you know when a student has met the outcome? What does that look like?" In many cases, the outcome itself will suggest the measurement tool. For example, if one of the outcomes is that students will use correct referencing style, an obvious measure is a student research paper that includes references. If a student outcome is focused on applying a particular theory to an example, the measurement might be a case study assignment that requires students to use a theory to analyze or develop a solution to the case. These types of assignments probably already exist in at least one course in the department. Faculty might choose to gather several of these into a portfolio, or they might pull individual assignments from particular courses that have a majority of students taking them. Some departments add a specific assignment to several courses in order to gather this information. Other measures that might be available are licensing or certification exams, jury evaluations, or internship supervisor reports. Again, these are the types of measures that are already embedded in the department's curricular offerings, and they are often direct measures of student learning.

Indirect measures of outcomes can provide a great deal of information to the department. Satisfaction surveys, alumni surveys, and even overall course evaluations might give some information to faculty about how well they are doing in terms of meeting the outcomes. Qualitative data can also provide a great deal of rich and complex information to students. Sometimes faculty believe that qualitative data are not "allowed" in an assessment planning process, but this type of information is often the most meaningful to faculty.

Following the identification of measures, the department is ready to move to phase 3 of the process: creation of a time line or calendar so that each outcome is measured regularly and departmental faculty know what data should be collected at what times during the semester. Some outcomes may not be measured each year, but they should be measured on a regular basis, and the department should clearly identify when they will be measured. This time line also allows for faculty to ensure that they work with students to get sufficient copies of papers that will be used for an assessment measure. Faculty must add the requirement to their syllabus before the actual paper is due so that students can comply with the request. This information is often included in the syllabus so that if two copies are required (one for the course and one for departmental assessment), students will know this in advance.

Phase 4 begins with measuring outcomes and collecting data. This will probably take place at various times of the academic year. Often a department has a single faculty member who is the assessment liaison and makes sure that everyone follows the time line.

Phase 5 is to analyze the data and share the findings with the faculty. Asking faculty to discuss the outcomes and whether they have been met, partially met, or not met is an excellent way to get the conversations started. For any outcome that was not clearly met, the department should discuss what types of action plans should be created so they can make modifications for the next year. This is the most important part of the process; without these discussions, transformation can never happen, and the assessment process becomes one of simple data collection. The departmental discussions about the findings and what to do about them are crucial. This is the information that the institution should want highlighted in all assessment plans. If a department reports that all of its outcomes were met and there are no action plans resulting from the process, it may be time to look more closely at the departmental outcomes. Is the target level too low? Are the outcomes too basic? Are all of their students really "ideal"?

The steps outlined so far focus on how departments can modify their existing outcomes and use them to strengthen learning and the student experience. All of this departmental work is important, and departments should be free to choose outcomes and measures that fit in with their disciplinary needs. However, some of the work done at the department level can also be used for the institutional-level assessment process.

The process of transformative assessment is often looked at as extending to the university as a whole, but departmental-level transformative assessment is where the most impact can be made. As departments discuss assessment findings and create action plans, they are the most able and the most likely to institute change at the course level. Departmental assessment should have an impact on what individual faculty members do within specific courses because the educational progress of students uses the individual course unit to help move a student from a first-year novice to a senior student with more advanced knowledge. Students may view taking courses as checking off requirements in order to get their degree, but there is real value in the viewing and practice of looking at the major as a path. Knowing where students are missing information and where this occurs can help the department implement change, but this change is most likely to occur within a specific course. Transformative assessment can provide meaningful information to make important teaching and learning modifications that will result in a difference.

As departments are developing their specific disciplinary-based outcomes, there is a possibility that many of these outcomes will reflect elements of the institutional mission. For example, if the institutional mission focuses on critical thinking, it is something that may play out at the department and course levels. Therefore, these individual departmental outcomes can and should be linked, where appropriate, to the overall institutional effectiveness plan. Data gathered from across campus, including academic and student affairs, can be used to determine how well the institution is meeting at least some of its goals. By using existing data from departments, the entire institution can look at aspects of its mission in an integrated way that does not require departments to develop outcomes that would not normally be created. In other words, faculty within departments and units still have complete control over their specific assessment plans, but elements of these plans can be aggregated and used to look across campus at broader effectiveness issues. This, then, is the sixth phase of the implementation process: using the data collected and analyzed to determine which outcomes need to have action plans created.

This approach to integrating the assessment analysis rather than assessment planning provides for a departmentally focused assessment plan that comes first, with the departmental assessment plans adding up to the institutional plan. This ground-up approach to creating assessment plans privileges the space where most of the academic learning occurs: in the classroom and in student support units that work directly with students.

Campuswide-Focused Model

A different approach to creating a transformative assessment plan is to look at the entire campus and build individual departmental and unit plans as part of the larger institutional plan. This process

can work well when there is not a strong departmental assessment program in place and the institution wants to incorporate
academic departments, student affairs units, and all other support
units into the whole assessment planning process.

Phase 1 of this implementation model begins with the mission
statement. Using the mission as a guide, the institution should
develop a set of institutional-level outcomes that align with the
mission and define its elements. Creating these institutional outcomes is a process that should involve broad participation across
the campus. Often a committee or task force is created that has
a representative from each of the major areas on campus, but it
should not be so large as to make decision making difficult. As
this committee creates a draft, there should be a communication
plan in place so that committee members can share the draft with
various constituencies and get feedback that can be used to refine
the draft. Getting faculty, staff, administration, and even student
involvement and leadership is essential. These outcomes should
have a shared buy-in across campus.

Once the institutional-level outcomes are in place, each department and support unit should be given a time frame in which to
create their specific outcomes. In phase 2 of the implementation,
departments and units work to make their outcomes align with
the institutional outcomes but still reflect their unique discipline
and content area. For example, the math department's outcomes
should be related to the math content, but the support unit for the
health center would have very different outcomes relating to its
specific charge. However, all units and departments could use some
of the same language and should certainly reflect the overall mission of the institution.

Phase 3 is to develop measures for both the institutional-level
outcomes and the departmental and unit outcomes. This can work
in any one of three ways. At some institutions, creating measures
for the institutional outcomes is done first. Once the institutional
measures are created, departments and units create measures for

their own specific outcomes. Because the institutional outcome measurements have already been chosen, some departments and units might decide to use some of those measures as their own. For example, if the overall institutional outcomes focus on critical thinking and use the Collegiate Learning Assessment (CLA) as an institutional measure, individual departments might also use the CLA for their students as a measure for departmental or unit critical thinking. This "double dipping" of measures may lead to better alignment and ensure that departments are not duplicating other measures already in place.

Other institutions may develop measures by asking the individual departments to complete this first and then move to creating institutional measures. The benefit to this sequence is that departmental measures will be specific to the disciplinary outcomes and may provide methods across campus for multiple measures of a group of outcomes. For example, if several departments have critical thinking as an outcome, they may create several mechanisms for measuring this within the content area. Then, when looking for institutional outcome measures, it becomes easier to gather all of the data on critical thinking that are already being measured within the departments. This makes it difficult to aggregate the data because of the different specifics of the measure, but the measures at the department level may prove to be more authentic and will certainly be specific to the content and context of the department and unit. A crucial piece of this third phase is that regardless of which set of measures is created first, the second set must be developed with knowledge of the first set. Otherwise duplication of effort is almost guaranteed. In order for the assessment process to be sustainable and meaningful, the process must be as streamlined as possible to get the most and best data possible without causing an unnecessary time commitment to this aspect of the process.

Phase 4 is to develop a time line that will show which outcomes and specific measures will be used and when. This phase is essential so that all involved will know which measures are to be given at what time. Explicitly stating the cycle of outcomes measurement will help to ensure that students are not asked to complete a large number of surveys or submit portfolios at a time when a lot of other data are being collected. This potentially multiyear time line or calendar of assessment will help all to see how the process will proceed.

Phase 5 occurs when the institution and departments begin to gather data using the measures that have been created. Since much of this information will be collected across the campus, a process should be in place to ensure that the data collected are stored appropriately and ready for analysis.

Phase 6 is to analyze the assessment data and share the findings across campus. Some of the information may be shared only with the departmental faculty or unit staff. These can be reported through an annual assessment report, but everyone needs to see all of the analyzed data. However, the analysis for the institutional level outcomes should be broadly shared.

Finally, phase 7 is to decide which outcomes were not appropriately met so that action plans at the department and institutional level can be created. This phase closes the feedback loop and allows for the intentional planning for institutional and departmental transformation.

Principles of Transformative Assessment

Based on the work of Jacqueline Moloney and Steven Tello (2003), transformative assessment can provide a framework for increasing the quality of higher education. Moloney and Tello specifically examined using assessment in online educational programs, but their work can certainly be used to better understand how transformative assessment should be part of an ongoing focus on quality education:

- Assessment is an ongoing and iterative process that should guide decision making to enhance the improvement of teaching and learning.

- Assessment outcomes and methods should be aligned with and guided by the institutional mission, goals, and outcomes.

- Assessment processes should engage members of the institution in an expanding spiral of participants that include faculty, staff, students, and the community.

- Assessment must be a process that collects, analyzes, and uses the data in an ethical and transparent way that will lead to continuous enhancement of student learning.

- Assessment across the institution provides opportunities for the identification of goals and outcomes and has a powerful potential to transform student learning, academic programs, and institutional practice.

As each institution develops and implements transformational assessment processes, following these principles will ensure that the outcomes are meaningful, the data collected worthwhile, and the analysis and action plans important.

Challenges and Lessons Learned

Several areas seem to regularly block the process of implementing transformative assessment. Knowing these pitfalls in advance can help to create a design that may lead to a faster and better development process.

One of these is a mismatch between the approaches to teaching and the process of assessment. When assessment is framed as a process required by outside others rather than as a method for modifying what is already occurring, many faculty and staff are likely to feel that their work is being questioned. Faculty who say, "You should trust me," are often demonstrating the belief that the assessment process is viewed as being separate and completely different from teaching and learning. When transformative assessment is presented as a process that is created and used by those who create it, individual departments and units may begin to see that they have ownership of assessment in the same way that they have ownership of the process of the curriculum. In addition, if transformative assessment can become part of the teaching-learning process, it is viewed more as part of the whole process. Few faculty members resist turning in final grades for students because this is part of the teaching process. In the same way, when faculty look to data on student learning in order to revise courses or reconsider curriculum and course sequencing, the system is designed to use assessment as a means for transformation.

Another area that often seems to be a barrier to transformative assessment is the belief that the findings from student learning assessment are going to be used punitively against a department or an individual faculty member. There must be sufficient trust among faculty and administration that will allow the collection of data that indicate areas where change is needed. Only by knowing where a department is not meeting outcomes can data-based decisions be made that will focus resources on areas that need them. The possibility of punitive action against a particular faculty member is especially an issue in small departments. For example, if only one faculty member is teaching the introductory course in a department and it is found that students are not well prepared for later courses, there is often a fear that that faculty member will be "blamed" for the problem. Rather than looking at the difficulty as a fault of the teaching or pedagogy, it is often helpful to look at the sequencing of topics through the syllabus. This allows a more objective look at the content without emphasizing that the course was taught by a single person.

Similarly, if assessment is seen only as something that comes at the end of the educational process and is summative in nature, transformation will be difficult. Assessment should be viewed as an ongoing and formative system that can inform teaching and learning at any time. By presenting transformative assessment as a formative system that helps to regularly align student learning with the teaching activities and programs, faculty and staff may feel that they do not necessarily have to create the "perfect" assessment plan. They may be more likely to feel comfortable beginning with a smaller number of outcomes and building the assessment system in a systematic, and thereby successful, way. Another aspect to this barrier is that often departments and units create an assessment plan and then consider their work done. A static assessment plan that measures the same outcomes year after year, however, will eventually be outgrown. The transformative assessment plan is dynamic, allowing modifications when necessary.

Thinking that assessment is best done with quantitative data is another challenge. Both qualitative and quantitative data can be used to directly measure student learning. Some outcomes may be better determined by qualitative measures, and some disciplines are more likely to use quantitative data. Neither one is inherently better. Faculty and staff should be able to use both tools to measure student outcomes.

When developing the implementation plan for transformative assessment, faculty must be involved from the beginning. Unfortunately many institutions begin the process of assessment at the administration level. When there is some push-back from faculty or staff, many administrators take on the task of developing the plan and inform the faculty and staff of the details later. However, faculty leadership is essential, and having broad-based participation is crucial. Assessment will be transformative only if the data can be analyzed and used to improve the educational process— and this educational process is most often in the hands of the faculty.

Implementing transformative assessment or modifying an existing assessment program takes time. Often institutions underestimate the actual amount of work and time that this will take in order to do it meaningfully and successfully. The reality is that transformative assessment is always a work in progress. Allowing the process to take enough time to make it accepted on a cross-campus basis but without becoming a quagmire of time and energy is a difficult line to walk. Only by going through the process and noting the progress can anyone be certain that the process is moving in the right direction. There will often be two steps back for every three steps forward, so the process can be frustrating. Having a core group of campus representatives working with the leadership of this implementation process can be extremely helpful in negotiating roadblocks and identifying problematic issues.

Another potential challenge to implementing transformative assessment is that often the perceived cause for action is an external mandate. When an institution views assessment mandates as being forced on it, it will often do the work, but not claim ownership or reap the rewards of potential information that can be useful. Framing the process, even when there is a need for accountability, as one that will inform and enlighten the institution is essential. Clearly it is good practice to collect and use information about student learning, and institutional leadership should provide that as the primary reason to use assessment as a transformative process.

Finally, problems will arise when there is a disconnect between assessment policies and actual practice. If assessment policy calls for due dates of plans that conflict with the academic calendar or if policy states that assessment results will not be used punitively but they are, the assessment will never become transformative. Policy and practice should align with the goal of gathering and using data to enhance student learning primarily, while also documenting the process as a secondary function. It is therefore important to bring new faculty, staff, and administrative members into this paradigm.

Sometimes a new dean, for example, may bring in expectations that are different from the existing institutional approach to transformative assessment. New members of the institutional community must be given sufficient information to ensure that certain policies are not violated that might break any trust in the process.

Implementing a transformative assessment process takes time. Institutions must commit to dialogue in many areas, from initial policy discussions through the analysis and use of data. And this dialogue must be ongoing: sharing data analysis and regularly assessing the work of the transformative assessment plan. Questions such as, "Is this still giving us the information that we need?" or "What else would be helpful to know in this area?" can help to guide the process and keep it from becoming static or stagnant. A well-implemented transformative assessment plan should be organic and flexible to meet the ever-changing needs of the institution and incorporate new outcomes and measures when appropriate.

8

Embedding Transformative Assessment
Activities Across the Institution

Most universities have data—a lot of data. And much of this information provides evidence of student learning. Consider all of the courses taught, exams given, projects graded, and in-class discussions held. All of these can and do give information about what and how much a student knows. The difficulty is that this information has typically been used for a single purpose: to assign a grade to an individual student within the context of a specific course. However, this information may be able to be used as a double-dip, providing evidence of individual student learning, as currently used, and documenting aggregate student learning across a department in ways that can inform the overall direction of teaching and curriculum design and provide for accountability in terms of student learning outcomes. The challenge is in choosing the appropriate elements from among the many that will provide the best evidence of student learning.

Being able to assess overall student learning outcomes while also providing information to faculty about individual student learning and giving students feedback about their own performance may seem like a dream come true. Using an authentic assessment tool can often do all of these things. And there is some evidence that the process of assessing student learning can actually enhance learning at the level of the individual student. "What and how students learn depends to a major extent on how they think they will be assessed" (Biggs, 1999, p. 141).

Authentic Forms of Assessment

Authentic assessment is an approach to measuring student learning that assesses specific student learning outcomes in the most direct and germane means possible. Because of this, authentic assessments are typically designed to promote the integration of content knowledge, higher-order thinking, problem solving, and application skills. These assessments are often based on actual student performance that asks students to apply particular course content to a problem situation or a real-life context. This assessment is typically an ongoing process within the structure of a course or project that results in some type of integrated work product. Grant Wiggins (1993) has stated that authentic assessment involves "engaging and worthy problems or questions of importance, in which students must use knowledge to fashion performances effectively and creatively. The tasks are either replicas of or analogous to the kinds of problems faced by adult citizens and consumers or professionals in the field" (p. 229).

The concept of authentic assessment has attracted a great deal of interest over the past several decades(Wilson & Sloane, 2000). It was often anticipated that authentic assessment practices would enable more reliable and meaningful information about student learning to be gathered. And that makes sense. If an institutional outcome focuses on the ability to problem-solve, what better way to measure it than to give students a problem and have them solve it? This would surely measure that outcome more reliably than giving a multiple-choice test on the process, for example. And if a department wanted students to develop good research skills, the best measure would clearly be requiring students to complete a research project. Authentic assessment can provide exciting and significant information about how well students are meeting learning outcomes.

Nevertheless, measuring student learning using authentic assessments has proven to be difficult. Part of the problem lies in the sheer numbers of students whose work must be assessed.

Measures of authentic assessment are time intensive in terms of the development of specific measures, management of the process, and overall data analysis. Also, the grading of so many different types of assignments presents a huge problem for comparability and grading standards across a department or institution. Students are often not used to this type of assignment, which presents another set of issues. It may take them longer to develop skills for demonstrating their knowledge with this type of assessment. "Initial hopes that alternative, authentic, or performance assessments of student achievement would drive (or at least facilitate) changes in what and how students are taught have been tempered by the realities of implementation" (Wilson & Sloane, 2000, p. 181).

But there are also advantages that may make the use of authentic assessment activities worth the time and energy required. Authentic assessment encourages students to integrate their knowledge and use information from across a course or even several courses to think through and develop a solution. This integration of content and critical thinking can be a powerful combination and can result in a much better prepared graduate. Also, authentic assessment assignments usually promote creativity. There is usually not a single correct answer; rather, the student must develop and analyze several possibilities before deciding on an appropriate course of action within the assignment. This can augment oral and written communication skills and collaboration and leadership skills, and it can better reflect the types of activities that a student may encounter once he or she enters the workforce.

John Mueller (2006) has indicated that authentic assessment is a process that helps to refine and modify the teaching curriculum. He uses the following example:

- A particular institution's mission is to develop productive citizens.
- To be a productive citizen, an individual must be capable of performing meaningful tasks in the real world.

- Therefore, schools must help students become proficient at performing the tasks they will encounter when they graduate.

- To determine if it is successful, the school must then ask students to perform meaningful tasks that replicate real-world challenges to see if students are capable of doing so.

It is therefore easy to see that the methods of developing these meaningful tasks will drive the sequencing and even the modification of the curriculum because the curriculum must facilitate specific student learning so that students can perform those tasks well. These types of authentic assessment tasks are often embedded within a particular course. "Alternative assessments, compared to traditional tests, offer the potential for greater ecological validity and relevance, assessment of a wider range of skills and knowledge, and adaptability to a variety of response modes" (Wilson & Sloane, 2000, p. 182). Because of this ecological validity, the data that result from this type of assessment are more likely to be used by individual faculty and even departments.

Embedded Assessment Practices

Embedded assessment is the term used when departments, programs, or even institutions collect data on student behavior or student learning for program or institutional-level assessment. It usually uses a process by which reviewers take a second look at materials created by students within a course or program to see what evidence they show concerning how well students have met specific learning outcomes (Palomba & Banta, 1999). Embedded assessment practices may also involve the creation of new exam questions, projects, or assignments that inform the individual instructor about a particular student's achievement level and give group-level information on the overall attainment of student learning associated with a major, a program, or even the entire institution.

Donald Farmer (1999) identified guidelines in creating and using embedded assessment. Faculty, he said, should:

- Understand curriculum as a plan for learning, not just a collection of courses that a student may check off a list.
- Provide sequential and cumulative learning throughout the course.
- Encourage transferable learning across the curriculum, including within a particular course and across a department or even the entire institution.
- Design the curriculum as a matrix by integrating the development of specific skill sets into the content of the courses.
- Implement student-centered teaching strategies to encourage engagement with the material and active rather than passive learning.
- Develop qualitative, performance-based, course-embedded assessment strategies both to assess and increase student learning and give this feedback to students so that they can better understand their own learning.
- Clearly define learning as the ability to apply prior learning to a new situation or context.

Benefits to Using Embedded Assessment

Using embedded assessment practices has several advantages. First, student data gathered from embedded assessment assignments or exams will be based on the developmental educational experiences of students. These types of authentic assessments have more ecological and instructional validity (Wilson & Sloane, 2000) and are more likely to benefit the faculty member as well as the student (Biggs, 1999). Faculty can use existing course-based assignments without having to create new methods of assessing learning. Students receive feedback on their assignments, faculty gain knowledge of student learning to use for grading, and the department can use student artifacts that are specific to program objectives and course requirements.

Second, embedded assessment often does not require any additional time for data collection, since these measures are already being used to indicate student learning within a specific course or required activity. This may mean that faculty do not feel as strongly that this process is being added to an already full schedule of teaching, scholarly work, and service. There will, however, be some additional time in the analysis of the data in order to use a particular course assignment to measure a departmental or unit outcome. However, once departments are used to gathering and using these data, it often becomes an integrated and necessary part of the decision-making process.

One department began using the final paper from the departmental senior seminar course as a method to evaluate student research skills. The faculty used the first faculty meeting of the next academic year to discuss the findings from the assessment committee members regarding the senior work. This process became so integrated into departmental life that even when a new department chair took over, the faculty wanted to see and discuss these findings each year so that they could use the information when they began to work with the current students.

Third, the presentation of feedback to faculty and students often happens in a relatively short period of time, so the data can be used in an ongoing and formative way. Also, since the specific embedded assessment assignment was created by faculty, there is a greater chance that they will use the results to bring about improvement. And because the embedded assessment project is closely linked to the curriculum and overall course or departmental goals, chances are greater that these assessment data will identify curricular areas that may need improvement. And, finally, embedded assessment is already being used for a student's grade, so there is a strong likelihood that it will be taken seriously by the student because each student will likely be motivated to perform to her or his best ability. Another related benefit of using course-embedded assessments is that they clearly tie what is taught with what is assessed. This alignment can bring increased validity to the process.

"The virtue of course-embedded assessment is that it puts assessment in the hands of faculty, rather than outside agencies. It yields data on student achievement that can be used to improve instruction" (Gerretson & Golson, 2005, p. 144). Clearly, course-embedded assessment has several benefits, but like any other assessment technique, some areas need to be addressed so that the implementation of specific course-embedded assessments can provide the necessary information with a time commitment that is appropriate.

Potential Challenges When Using Embedded Assessment

Faculty must understand that the intent when using embedded assessment practices is not to second-guess the teaching abilities or grading practices of the faculty, but to focus on the information gathered regarding student learning. This may be one of the most widely accepted beliefs regarding the use of this type of assessment. In using any type of assessment, faculty must be confident that they are not going to be compared to other faculty in terms of teaching abilities. Without this level of trust, faculty are less likely to participate, and if they are mandated to participate, they may begin to believe that their academic freedom is being infringed on because of the mandate. Assessment of any kind, especially transformative assessment, will not work without a sense of trust and consensus established on campus in terms of how the data will be used.

Faculty commitment to creating and using embedded assessment is essential. But this can sometimes be difficult to ensure, so faculty resistance may be considerable. Trust is an important factor, but even with a sense of trust established, faculty may still resist committing to the process. Embedded assessment must first and foremost be meaningful and appropriate for assessing student performance within the class. This gives the assessment tool some instructional validity (Wilson & Sloane, 2005). Faculty will be more likely to use an assignment that is already in place than to try to create one to add to their course that will also meet a departmental or other assessment need. Faculty must also be able to see the value in using this tool and view the resulting information as valuable for others. "Every assessment is also based on a set of beliefs about the kinds of tasks or situations that will prompt students to say, do, or create something that demonstrates important knowledge and skills. The tasks to which students are asked to respond on an assessment are not arbitrary" (National Research Council, 2001, p. 47). As the institution begins to move toward using additional embedded assessment tools, the different course content and context issues must be acknowledged and respected.

Another potential problem in using this process is that there is often no way to compare data across courses or even sections of the same course. This comparability issue must be settled prior to the use of this process. According to Mark Wilson and Kathryn Sloane (2000), "On a logistical level, using open-ended or performance-based tasks require different procedures for collecting, managing, and scoring student work. Records of performances must be catalogued and stored. Responses can no longer be scanned by machine and entered directly into a statistical database. Raters must score the work, and to do so raises issues of time and cost as well as technical issues involved in rater fairness (e.g., consistency and reliability)" (p. 196). One of the strengths of using embedded assessment activities is that they are authentic learning tasks; however, this also becomes one of the challenges. Trying to aggregate data across courses or even disciplines can be difficult and, based on the specific assignments, perhaps even impossible. Therefore, the choice of which type of embedded assessment tool to use must be made in advance so that any potential difficulties in comparing data across several courses are worked out in advance.

Designing Embedded Measures

Once an institution or a program has determined that it will be using some embedded assessment measures, there are specific steps that should be followed in order to make the best use of the data collected. Often it is not necessary to design a new assessment process; several measures will already be in place within the courses in the major. The difficulty is often in choosing which measures to use and how to analyze the data on a program or department level.

The first step is to determine the specific learning objectives for the program or department so that all are considering the same area that needs the embedded measure. If a department wants to measure student research skills, all faculty can look at their courses to see what assignments may be in place that might demonstrate the level of student learning for this outcome. It may be that the department chooses to look at a couple of measures for this outcome: one in an introductory course and one in a later course. By doing this, it will be possible to look at student development within this learning outcome. Even if only one measure is to be used, the department must, if it has not already done so, determine how those outcomes are translated into the individual courses taught within the program. This process, typically called *curriculum mapping*, can demonstrate which courses are meeting specific outcomes.

By using curriculum mapping as a way to organize the overall outcomes of individual courses, faculty can more clearly understand and graphically see the intended learning outcomes and how they are introduced and taught through the curriculum. In addition, faculty can more easily see what material needs to be emphasized to ensure that students are taught concepts and content in a particular order and that prerequisite courses introduce the material appropriately. Curriculum mapping can also promote higher quality as new courses are created because specific connections among outcomes and course topics can be intentionally organized. In addition, curriculum mapping will more easily show how to align assessment plans to the overall structure of the departmental curriculum, which will better ensure that student learning is assessed in the most meaningful and appropriate way possible. Finally, as faculty revise courses and lessons, curriculum mapping can best demonstrate which areas need additional emphasis and which are covered in many courses. A curriculum map is typically designed as a matrix (see Table 8.1) with the courses on one axis and the outcomes on another. Faculty can then identify which outcomes are introduced or studied at an advanced level for each course that is taught.

Once the specific outcomes are identified, the department or program should conduct an inventory of the types of assignments that are already being used within the various courses. This could be a listing of assignments that might demonstrate student learning for each of the outcomes or a listing of student work products by course. Either way, the department faculty should be able to view how the learning outcomes are already being assessed

Table 8.1. A Curriculum Map

	Course Title 1	Course Title 2	Course Title 3	Course Title 4
Outcome 1		Introduced		
Outcome 2			Advanced	Advanced
Outcome 3	Introduced	Advanced		
Outcome 4	Introduced			

at the individual student level within each course. Following this, the faculty must decide which assignments would best be used for program-level assessment purposes. Some of the assignments might be able to be used as is, but some might need some modification, and this must be discussed fully to make certain that each assignment will prove meaningful and useful.

When the assessment tools are agreed on, they must be integrated into the course as embedded assessments. In doing this, it is often helpful to create a department-level calendar or time line to provide a clear picture of what will be collected, by whom, and when during the academic year. As part of this process, faculty must decide the format in which they want these student work products submitted. Some departments ask students to turn in two copies of the assignment: one is graded for the course, and the other is kept for assessment. Some departments ask that the assessment copy be submitted without the student name so that it can later be reviewed blind. Departments that have students submit items electronically can create an electronic folder or portfolio of assignments for later departmental or program assessment.

Once the data are gathered, faculty must plan the methods for analyzing the embedded assessments. This can be a difficult part in the process, especially in small departments with only one or two faculty. Some faculty are wary about having student work that is done in their courses read by others in the department. This can be especially true if the faculty member is untenured. Sensitivity to the way data are analyzed and given to the department is crucial if trust in the process is to be maintained.

Once the data have been collected and analyzed, the departmental assessment committee can determine the areas of strengths and weaknesses of the students as demonstrated by the embedded assessments.

Finally, the feedback circle must be closed. The department must use the data to make transformations and appropriate changes to the curriculum if indicated by the data or modify the assessments if they do not provide the information needed. Because using embedded assessment is going to provide increased instructional validity and the content is clearly aligned with the assessment process, it is more likely that the embedded assessment data will be used to make meaningful changes. Also, because of the nature of embedded assessment assignments, the process is probably going to be more easily sustained and will be viewed by the faculty as useful data.

This process will work only when the assessment is designed carefully and intentionally. The creation of the embedded assessment is crucial if the data collected will be meaningful, useful, and valid. Each assignment must first meet the needs of the course. What specific behaviors or skills should the student demonstrate? What are the ways that these can be shown? The data that are collected are only as good as the assignment is. Care should be taken to ensure that the assignment chosen by the department from within a particular course will provide the information needed to assess the outcomes agreed on.

Here are some examples of course-based embedded assessments:

- Questions embedded within final exams
- Common questions embedded in exams across course sections
- Pre- and posttests
- Rubrics used to grade a class project, presentation, or performance
- Samples of student work such as a project or paper
- Elements of a portfolio
- Field or other internships
- Some form of authentic assessment, such as a music performance or written work submitted to a journal

Outside-the-Classroom Activities

This chapter has focused almost entirely on embedded assessment techniques within academic courses, majors, and programs. But embedded assessment can also be a part of transformative assessment in programs that may have activities that occur outside the classroom. One of the largest areas on most campuses that fits into this category is that of student affairs. As is often the case, many of the programs and projects that happen within these cocurricular activities are not tied directly to a particular course. Nevertheless, they often yield student products that can demonstrate student knowledge of and development toward particular institutional or unit ideals.

The same basic process will work in the development of embedded assessment activities within nonclassroom-based programs. Identifying the overall goals and outcomes is a first and necessary step. Following this, a process similar to curriculum mapping can take place. The same matrix shown in Table 8.1 can be used to determine what projects and student work are available to be used. Student leadership plans, student work with specific cocurricular organizations, and even programming done within residence halls are all potential sources of student learning data.

Modifying Syllabi to Reflect Learning Outcomes

The course syllabus should reflect embedded assignments. An assessment of individual student learning within a course for which a student receives points toward a final grade will certainly increase the motivation to perform well. By identifying these assignments in the syllabus as important, both students and faculty will recognize that a particular assignment is an important part of the course. Students do not necessarily need to know that this assignment will be used for overall departmental assessment, but students should see clearly how that assignment is aligned with the overall course outcomes and that the course outcomes are aligned with the overall mission of the department or major.

The syllabus, of course, provides information to the student about course content, activities and assignments, and often the instructor's expectations, policies, and procedures for the course. It usually identifies what will be taught and when it will be taught, when specific assignments will be due, how assignments and exams are used to calculate grades, and other information regarding attendance and participation in class, late assignments, missed exams, and academic misconduct, for example.

A syllabus that is organized and complete signals to students that the instructor is prepared, cares about student learning, and will create effective learning experiences. Faculty can also benefit from a well-constructed syllabus because when students are given specific information about the course and the expectations for participation and assignments, they may better understand the rationale for assignments and exams; therefore, they may perform better and ask fewer questions about due dates and procedures. When an assignment that will be used for departmental-level assessment is embedded in the course, it is especially important that students follow the assignment carefully and are motivated to perform well. There also may be additional instructions for that assignment. For example, students may need to turn in multiple copies of the assignment or may need to submit one copy in electronic format. All of these details should be made explicit in the syllabus.

Principles of Embedded Assessment Systems

Kathryn Sloane, Mark Wilson, and Sara Samson (1996) have identified four principles to use when focusing on an embedded assessment plan. These principles, they say, were "standards or ideals that should, we believed, be reflected in a technically-sound, curriculum-embedded, classroom-based system of student assessment" (p. 5).

The first principle is that the assessment process should acknowledge and demonstrate that students gain information in developmental ways. In other words, students' knowledge and skills will develop over time, and an appropriate assessment strategy should measure at intervals to demonstrate this development. According to Sloane et al., "A developmental perspective helps us move away from 'one shot' testing situations, and away from cross sectional approaches to defining student performance—toward an approach that focuses on the process of learning and on an individual's progress through that process" (p. 6).

The second principle is that of instructional fidelity. This focuses on the need to better align the assessment instrument and the instructional techniques. Unfortunately most assessment practices do not align well with instructional methods and pedagogy. Students may, for example, report that they studied for a test but were surprised by the content and knowledge that were actually tested. This might be an indication that a student was not prepared, but it could also be a sign that the testing and assessment methods did not match what was taught. "The rationale for the development of 'authentic' or 'alternative' or 'performance' assessment techniques is based, at its heart, on the need for a better match between important learning objectives (e.g., 'problem solving') and the methods by which student performance on these objectives is assessed" (Sloane et al., 1996, p. 6).

The third principle for effective embedded assessment systems is that of teacher management and responsibility. Faculty have the responsibility of creating these embedded assessment assignments and analyzing them so that the information can be used to benefit student learning. This can happen on both the course and department levels. Faculty must also manage the amount of information that is collected. Because of this, faculty must have the authority to choose the type of assignment. According to Sloane et al. (1996), "Teachers must be the managers of the system, and hence must have the tools to use it efficiently and use the assessment data effectively and appropriately" (p. 7).

The final principle is that of the quality of the evidence collected. "It is not sufficient that alternative forms of assessment should express new ideas of validity, they must also maintain the standards of fairness (such as consistency and unbiasedness) that have been accepted as standards for traditional assessments" (Sloane et al., 1996, p. 7). As new embedded assessment methods are created and used, the departmental faculty must be assured that the data are valid and reliable evidence of student learning. The type of evidence that is often collected with embedded assignments tends to be rich, complex, and filled with information that goes beyond what is actually needed to measure a specific outcome. The quality of the evidence and the data analysis is very important if the resulting assessment data are going to be accepted and used for transformation.

Conclusion

Using appropriate, valid, and reliable embedded-assessment assignments can provide the data that will enable a department or unit to make modifications that will contribute even more to student learning. Because these assignments are often well aligned with the overall departmental and course outcomes and because students will be more motivated to perform well for an assignment grade, using embedded assessment can provide excellent transformative assessment data. Embedded assessment procedures can also make the integration of the assessment process with teaching and learning more significant, which will encourage the use of the data for improving the educational outcomes for students.

9

Transformative Assessment as a Method to Support Ongoing Accreditation and Accountability

"C an assessment for accountability and assessment for improvement coexist? Can the current accountability focus actually strengthen assessment for improvement? Or will an accountability tidal wave roll across the fields, crushing the fragile green sprouts of assessment for improvement that have begun to appear?" These questions posed by Trudy Banta (2007b, p. 9) succinctly identify the tension that exists between accountability and transformation as the result of assessment efforts.

Assessment for the purpose of accountability is clearly an important issue for maintaining accreditation at individual institutions. Without the push from accreditors, assessment would never have gained the growth that it has in the past twenty-five to thirty years. Decisions made by regional and specialized accreditors have caused institutions to begin to take very seriously the need to identify outcomes, measure them appropriately, and use the results to improve the institution in general and student learning specifically. However, with the now common and widely acknowledged need for assessment offices and directors and a clearer focus on measuring student learning, there is also a cost. This top-down approach to mandating assessment has created many institutions that are not pursuing assessment as a means for higher quality but as a necessary path to maintain accreditation. "Most institutions think about assessment now as a means to appease the accreditors, not necessarily as a way to learn about their own institutions, because the stakes have become so high" (Schilling, 2006, p. 2).

Accountability as a Secondary Purpose of Assessment

The primary purpose of any assessment plan is focused on student learning. It "is the systematic collection, review, and use of information about educational programs undertaken for the purpose of improving student learning and development" (Palomba & Banta, 1999, p. 4). Another definition of assessment is that it is the "process of gathering and discussing information from multiple and diverse sources in order to develop a deep understanding of what students know, understand, and can do with their knowledge as a result of their educational experiences; the process culminates when assessment results are used to improve subsequent learning" (Huba & Freed, 2000, p. 8). Mary Allen (2004) states that "as a whole, assessment is a framework for focusing faculty attention on student learning and for provoking meaningful discussions of program objectives, curricular organization, pedagogy, and student development" (p. 4). None of these well-accepted definitions of assessment includes any information about collecting information for accountability purposes. The focus is on improving and enhancing student learning.

As a part of the assessment process, data that outside accreditors and others in the public request will also be collected. This information collected for use by the institution is often used to document the work of the institution and provide data on accountability. Using this secondary purpose of assessment, that of accountability, assessment can also be seen as "any effort to gather, analyze, and interpret evidence which describes institutional, divisional or agency effectiveness" (Upcraft & Schuh, 1996, p. 18). The description of institutional effectiveness for external use is certainly an important issue, and few institutions can afford to ignore its importance.

But the focus on student learning should always be the primary purpose of any transformative assessment process. It has been said that "you can't steer the boat by watching the wake," and this is certainly applicable to institutions of higher education. Knowing how much students are learning so that accreditors or others in the public will be satisfied is just a small part of the overall process of assessment. By focusing only on the outcomes that will be reported, institutions run the risk of measuring only those areas that they are certain will make the institution look good. Looking at the mission and keeping that as the driving force behind the transformative assessment process is crucial to the ongoing progress and increased effectiveness of any institution, department, program, or even individual course. Assessments should be created to improve learning rather than to document to others the success of the institution.

The process of a good assessment program (Palomba & Banta, 1999, p. 16):

- Asks important questions
- Reflects institutional mission
- Reflects programmatic goals and objectives for learning
- Contains a thoughtful approach to assessment planning
- Is linked to decision making about the curriculum
- Is linked to processes such as planning and budgeting
- Encourages involvement of individuals from on and off campus
- Contains relevant assessment techniques
- Includes direct evidence of learning
- Reflects what is known about how students learn
- Shares information with multiple audiences

- Leads to reflections and action by faculty, staff, and students

- Fosters continuity, flexibility, and improvement in assessment

Although many of these characteristics can be seen as useful in terms of accountability, the obvious primary focus is on measuring student learning and using the information for continuous enhancement.

Role of Regional Accreditors

Assessment has become a part of almost all institutions of higher education in the United States because of regional accreditation. Without the initial requirements mandating the implementation of assessment, many institutions would not be practicing any form of outcomes assessment. Regional accreditors also play an important part in working with the U.S. government in terms of setting policies and assuring the public that higher education is doing what it should be doing. Interestingly, institutions often view the regional accreditor as a negative influence on the functioning of the university. However, because they often act as a buffer between individual institutions and the governmental process, regional accreditors are actually working for higher education in general. The standards, criteria, and principles that are in place in regional accrediting agencies are meant to ensure quality and encourage ongoing institutional self-study and the resulting improvement while being adaptive enough to be used across the great variety of U.S. higher education institutions.

There has certainly been criticism of the existing accreditation system. Secretary of Education Margaret Spellings said in a speech to the National Press Club, "Right now, accreditation is the system we use to put a stamp of approval on higher-education quality. It's largely focused on inputs—more on how many books are in a college library than whether students can actually understand them. Institutions are asked, 'Are you measuring student learning?' And they check yes or no. That must change. Whether students are learning is not a yes-or-no question" (U.S. Department of Education, 2006b). Other frustrations with the accreditation system come from institutions that have gone through or are preparing for the accreditation process (Alstete, 2004). Some have said that the process is unclear and complex. In discussing a report from the American Council of Trustees and Alumni, Jeffrey Alstete (2004) wrote that "although accreditation began as a voluntary system to set good standards and identify quality schools, it was evolved into a false stamp of government-approved quality that is required for all institutions that wish to offer federal financial aid" (pp. 20–21).

However, the process of accreditation has been the driving force behind much of the institutional-level change in higher education:

> Many stakeholders—including colleges, policymakers, and the accreditors themselves—defend the basics of the existing system by arguing that institutional accreditation is inevitably complex and must stay flexible if it is to achieve its many goals. Institutions vary significantly in terms of capacity, goals, missions, and operations, making the establishment of benchmarks and standards difficult, even counterproductive. The key in accreditation, they argue, is to find a balance: setting standards that can guide the institutional review process in clear directions, while preserving institutions' individual missions and objectives [Biswas, 2006, pp. 1–2].

Finding the right balance is difficult. Institutions across the United States are often very different from one another. Size, levels of student preparedness, demographics, and even geographical location cause institutions to have unique needs, goals, and outcomes. Regional accrediting standards have to be able to over-lay the many different types and systems of institutions while still having the ability to come to some type of decision about overall quality.

Regional accreditation agencies have been making modifica-tions to their standards for over a decade, including explicit require-ments about measuring student learning and overall institutional effectiveness. These changes have been difficult to make, and many institutions have had to construct organizational and policy changes to keep up with the mandates of accreditation. However, it is possible to use the accreditation process as a lever to encour-age institutional leaders to focus on student learning and the actual skills and behaviors that students will gain at a particular institution.

An example of recent changes can be seen in one of the compre-hensive standards for the Commission on Colleges of the Southern Association of Colleges and Schools (SACS): "The institution identifies expected outcomes for its educational programs (includ-ing student learning outcomes for educational programs) and its administrative and educational support services, assesses whether it achieves these outcomes, and provides evidence of improvement based on analysis of those results" (SACS Comprehensive Standard 3.3.1). This standard has now made it necessary for all institutions accredited by SACS to have student learning outcomes for all edu-cational programs, administrative programs, and support areas, and they must measure those outcomes and use the resulting informa-tion for enhancing the entire institution.

It is fair to say that most universities would not necessarily do this type of work across the institution if this requirement were not in place. Therefore, the accreditation process has caused a need to put these types of practices in place. The specific standards and requirements of regional accreditation bodies effect change at the institutional level and thus often guide the modifications made in higher education. However, the member institutions that are affected by regional accreditation are also the ones that make the system work: members of institutions vote as delegates on policy changes at the regional level, serve as reviewers and evaluators for both off- and on-site accreditation visits, and create the direction that regional accreditation will go. Regional accreditation is not something that is "done to" an institution. Rather, it relies on the institutions within the geographical area to make the system work. And it has worked well for many years.

Unfortunately, many faculty and some administrators would be very happy to see an end to regional accreditation because of the many rules and the sometimes expensive and difficult methods for complying with these rules. However, if this were to happen, there would still have to be some sort of oversight of higher education, and that would come directly from the U.S. government. There have been some discussions about a No Child Left Behind type of policy for postsecondary education, and this would almost certainly cause more distress than the regional accreditation system.

Local Institutional Assessment and Transformation

Transformative assessment works best when the process is developed by those who will eventually use the resulting data for decision making. This process is, by definition, fundamentally a local one. The faculty, staff, administration, and students within the institution are the ones who must be responsible for designing the assessment system to provide information that is needed, meaningful, and appropriate. As Mike Theall (personal communication, 2008) has said, "All evaluation and development are local."

To some, there may be an interesting juxtaposition of local, transformative assessment with the concept of regional, state, or even national accreditation standards. How can something designed by a national or regional accreditation committee be used for local, transformative assessment? Ralph Wolff, executive director of the Senior College Commission of the Western Association of Schools and Colleges, said that accreditors have put the responsibility for assessment on "an institution to define its learning outcomes, and to assess the achievement of those outcomes and through that assessment to determine whether improvement is needed" (reported by Lederman, 2007, para. 9). Trudy Banta (2007b) puts it even more succinctly: "We must work together with our stakeholders to make assessment for improvement and assessment for accountability complement, even strengthen, one another" (p. 12).

Accreditation standards do play a large role in determining what is measured and what becomes important for reporting on local university and college campuses. But they are not the only outside influence over institutional policy and practices. Consider the perceived importance of the *U.S. News and World Report* rankings each year or the data requested by the Integrated Postsecondary Education Data System (IPEDS). Any change to the IPEDS reporting requirements will immediately cause individual institutional research offices to change what they measure and how they report it. Accreditation requirements are only one example, albeit an important one, of how outside forces can cause local campuses to modify what and how they measure.

But how the local institution chooses to modify policy and practice is something that is based on the individual campus culture, leadership, and institutional members. Accreditation requirements, while relatively structured, leave many of the specifics to be defined and developed locally. Because of this flexibility, it is possible for assessment for accountability and assessment for transformation to occur simultaneously, using the same outcomes, measures, and findings.

Assessing for Accountability or Airing Dirty Laundry?

Even the concept of airing dirty laundry from an institution implies that something in the data should be hidden. This goes against the entire principle of transformative assessment.

Transformative assessment is geared toward finding out what is not working well so that more attention, resources, and thought can be given to that area. If instead a problem area is seen as something that must be hidden, the opportunity to grow and transform is lost. Higher education needs to get past the notion that not doing well must be kept secret at all costs. Knowing where a specific institution is not reaching its desired outcome should instead be something that is celebrated because that is one of the only paths that will lead to change.

Sharing this information publicly, however, can be detrimental to other areas of institutional life. Senior administrators tend to dislike going public with information about their institution that is negative, and that might dissuade students from applying or returning to the campus. How can higher education get past this seemingly impossible dichotomy?

Significance of the Audience

Information about an institution's areas of weakness (or opportunities, as they are sometimes euphemistically called) is collected primarily for the purpose of internal analysis. Discussions on what should be changed will happen more easily when there is a clear area that needs to be modified and widespread agreement on the problem. For transformation to occur, of course, the problem must be identified and solutions created that will address the situation. When the audience is not the internal institutional constituents, knowing what is not working may not be as important as knowing what modifications have been made for improvement. Therefore, not every bit of data needs to be shared widely outside the campus. However, sharing new initiatives or programs based on areas that need additional support can be useful to the general public. In other words, an internal report may include all of the details, while the information that goes up on the institutional Web site may focus solely on the new program or the changes to an existing one. The focus here is not on "spinning," but on acknowledging that different audiences have different needs for information.

For example, one institution has in its mission statement an area focusing on ethical decision making. This institution also has begun to look at developing an explicit student honor code. In preparation, it surveyed students to determine the level of academic dishonesty. There was, as might be imagined, some concern about what would happen if the survey indicated a high level of dishonesty among students. How would that information look to the board? Parents of current students? Potential students? Employers? The decision was made to distribute the survey and see what the data indicated. This institution decided that it was better to know than to guess about what was actually occurring. Although the initial data might indicate a higher level of academic dishonesty than anyone was comfortable with, knowing where the issues were made it possible for the institution to make changes in pedagogy, assignment creation, and faculty development and to add an academic integrity portion to the orientation for incoming students. By tracking these data, this institution was able to see that the changes did indeed make a difference. It was better off in the long run by collecting information that at first could have been potentially damaging. Because transformative assessment is an ongoing process, the institution can surmount these types of individual weak areas knowing that improvements will happen and institutional effectiveness will increase.

Importance of Language

How language is used can make a big difference when information is being shared. Several terms that are commonly used in higher education may not be clear to others and, in some cases, may actually mean something different. If, for example, an institution that is accredited by the Commission on Colleges of the Southern Association of Colleges and Schools (SACS) receives a "recommendation," those within the institution know that this means that there is an area where the institution is not in compliance and must change. For those outside higher education, however, "recommendation" may mean that it is merely a suggestion and not something that must be addressed. Even the word *assessment* has many different meanings, and this can cause confusion. Knowing how an audience might define terms is essential for clear understanding and good communication.

The potential solution to this issue is to make certain that information shared is clear, concise, and written in a language that everyone will understand. This means using no jargon or acronyms. Most in higher education understand SAT and ACT scores and would be pleased to know that their incoming first-year students had an average 23 ACT score. But to external stakeholders, this may be meaningless information. Stating instead that the incoming first-year students were above average on a national standardized test may be exactly the information that they need.

Transparency of the Process

Regardless of how terms are used, transparency in the reporting process is crucial. If the members of the institution and the general public are going to have trust that the institutional reporting process is sound, there must be some level of transparency about the assessment process. Information must be included that indicates the time line, the overall goals, the methods used to gather data, the general results, and decisions made regarding the results. While the same level of detail may be very different depending on the report's intended audience, there should always be sufficient transparency communicated about the overall process.

Just as a student wants to know how a paper's grade will be determined, the overall institution should indicate how the information it is sharing was gathered and how the institution is interpreting the results. Hiding data because they do not show the institution in the best light is almost always sure to be discovered.

And this discovery will certainly make some believe that other pieces of important information were not disclosed either.

Institutional Preparation for Accreditation: Flossing Teeth

Marcus Jorgenson (2007) compared the practice of flossing teeth to the ongoing practice of assessment. He indicated that most people—even those who do not regularly floss—will not argue against the need for flossing teeth regularly. Similarly, most cannot dispute the fact that ongoing measurement of student learning and the use of that information to inform teaching, learning, and institutional practices can have a positive impact on the institution. Those who do not floss are likely to have painful gums, difficult visits to the dentist, and the possible loss of teeth.

Taking this analogy to assessment, institutions that are not regularly assessing student learning have lost opportunities to improve, the potential of more governmental control, and the potential of losing accreditation, and therefore federal funding. However, with regular flossing, an individual has healthy gums and pain-free dental visits. In the same vein, institutions that continuously assess student learning will have an increased and positive impact on students and less strenuous preparation for visiting accreditation teams.

Just as an individual cannot fake long-term flossing, an institution cannot recreate the assessment work that should have been done over previous years. "One of the dangers of focusing on reviews by accrediting agencies is neglecting assessment and then trying to make up for lost time by engaging assessment activities as the institution's ten-year review approaches (Schilling, 2006, p. 2). This type of institutional push for assessment will typically lead only to assessment for accountability and will teach faculty and staff that it is being done only for the outside accreditors. Nothing is more likely to derail any potential benefits gained from assessing student learning.

Conclusion

Transformative assessment is a local process that can support and be supported by regional and specialized accreditation. They are not mutually exclusive. The assessment process will certainly vary from institution to institution even within the same geographical and regional accreditation system. Even public institutions within a statewide system may demonstrate different outcomes, measures, and analysis of findings.

In order for this process to be effective, however, institutional faculty, administration, and trustees must take responsibility for the institutional effectiveness process. There must be a shared sense of purpose and a high level of integrity in ensuring honesty when developing and reporting on the levels of effectiveness. Individual institutions and their constituent community members must take seriously their role in ensuring the ongoing quality enhancement process of an institution. Going beyond the easily measured and the typical benchmarking methods is crucial. No institution is perfect, and all need to focus on what needs to be transformed in order to better prepare students according to its mission and goals. Individuals within the higher education community must be advocates for the process of ongoing accreditation decision making. This level of service should be expected and rewarded for all levels of staff and faculty. While not every member of a campus community can or should participate as evaluators in on-site evaluation visits, all should support and contribute to the local institution and even the national process in any way that is appropriate.

Higher education and the overall accreditation process is a means to contribute to institutional effectiveness. It is a process that has developed over time and continues to improve. It allows the self-regulation of individual campuses, yet in a way to assure the general public that overall higher education in the United States is outstanding, responsive to changing needs, and a precious commodity to be treasured.

10

The Future of Transformative
Assessment in Higher Education

Higher education will be using assessment for accountability and transformation for many years to come. What will change are the methods that will be used to measure student learning and the emphasis placed on specific outcomes. "While virtually all states currently report on collegiate learning using proxies e.g. graduation rates, colleges and universities are now being asked to assess learning directly" (Shavelson, 2007b, p. 26). Assessment practices should work within the educational system, benefiting both the institution and the students who are demonstrating their learning. The process that is designed and modified should become more integrated into the systems of higher education. Essentially effective assessment is either going to create action or confirm current practices (Swing, 2004).

This is all assuming, of course, that assessment becomes more effective. There is a great interest in the oversimplified and "easy" version of assessment that will want to test all students on the same exam and then demonstrate which institution is "best" in terms of student learning. This approach, however, has major problems, and it will not benefit those whom it purports to help. One of the recommendations made by the Commission on the Future of Higher Education (U.S. Department of Education, 2006a) was that the "collection of data from public institutions allowing meaningful interstate comparison of student learning should be encouraged and implemented in all states" (p. 24). There are many problems with this approach. Trudy Banta (2007b) states that "the commercially available tests of these abilities that I have studied recently are surprisingly lacking in vital information about their reliability and validity" (p. 10). Transformative assessment is unlikely to occur if the significant measure that is used measures a small sample of students on a small sample of their knowledge and performance. If assessment is going to be used to benefit higher education, it must be done at the local level, following a process that is appropriate, meaningful, sustainable, flexible and ongoing and will harness the data for improvement with the potential for substantive change.

In order for transformative assessment to work within the context of postsecondary education and provide data that will enable institutions to make positive and meaningful changes, certain issues must be understood and in some cases developed further. These issues are discussed in more detail in the remaining parts of this chapter.

Increasing Accountability and Comparability Needs

There have been continued calls for more accountability in higher education. Accreditation is just one area that is requiring information from individual institutions demonstrating elements of institutional effectiveness. There will be an increase in the need to document what an institution is doing in terms of learning, job placement, and mission-related activities:

> The nation's educational competitiveness continues to slip, particularly in diploma and degree production. Higher education prices continue to rise, leading stakeholders to increasingly question the value of higher education's product. The evolution of the standards movement in elementary and secondary education, exemplified by the No Child Left Behind Act, raises important and controversial questions

about the purpose, scale, and scope of learning assessment [American Association of State Colleges and Universities, 2006, p. 3].

With the development of several large-scale tests, such as the National Survey of Student Engagement and the Collegiate Learning Assessment (CLA), the promise of effective benchmarking, reduced resources, and the public call for more information, many institutions are moving toward giving exams and sharing information. Previously much of the information used to compare institutions was focused on aspects of the institution, such as retention and graduation rates, funding per student, student-to-faculty ratio, faculty publications, and grant funding amounts. Now, with large-scale tests that measure elements of student learning, institutions can gather information specific to program or even overall institutional goals. When, for example, a sample of students at an institution take the CLA, their scores can be compared with those of students at other institutions. Is this a better way to compare institutional effectiveness? Perhaps it is better than knowing how many average dollars a department brings in from external grants.

Since comparisons can be made among institutions that are participating in these large-scale tests, many are doing just that. However, as Banta has often pointed out, given the high rates of correlation between some of these tests and SAT scores, there is very little variability that can occur because of the specific institution that a student attends. In other words, only a small part of the overall variance is due to what actually happens to a student in college. The Association of American Colleges and Universities (2006) has stated:

Given the new emphasis on standardized testing in the schools, many observers are asking whether such testing should now become the gold standard for quality assessment in higher education. On educational grounds, AAC&U has taken a stand against the view that standardized tests are the best way to assess students' learning gains and level of accomplishment over their several years in college. AAC&U does believe, however, that standardized tests can supplement curriculum-embedded assessments when they are used with appropriate professional standards and cautions [p. 10].

Regardless, there is an increasingly strong demand for accountability and comparison across institutions.

Higher education cannot stick its collective heads in the sand and wait for this call to end. It probably will not. What might happen, however, is that a series of tests and measurements may be created and required of all institutions. Rather than wait for this to happen, those in higher education need to work to develop and use appropriate tests and make certain that they are used in valid ways. "U.S. educators need to lobby for the installation of instructionally sensitive accountability tests. They can do so by first learning more about such tests and then using whatever energy and influence they have to urge key policymakers to install more indefensible accountability tests" (Popham, 2006, p. 83).

Changing Student Matriculation Patterns

Characteristics of the typical college student are changing. Students are "stopping out" more often: they are beginning their college career, leaving for a time, and then returning to complete their degree. And many students are taking courses at multiple locations and transferring them to a variety of institutions prior to graduating from a single institution.

These changing patterns of student retention can violate some of the underlying assumptions about assessing student learning. Many departmental and even institutional-level assessment plans are predicated on the concept that a student comes to the institution, that institution causes learning to happen, and then the student's learning is measured. However, when students move between institutions, they are often not included in some of the assessment measures that are used. And if there are pre- and post-test measures as part of the assessment plan, it is unlikely that a transfer student will be on campus to participate in the pretest. It might be assumed that an institution with higher posttest scores on a given measure was demonstrating an increase in student learning that is likely caused by the institutional impact on the student. However, if there is a percentage of students who have left the institution and a new cohort of transfer students has entered, the assumption that the pretest and posttest can be compared is certainly an issue.

As students move from institution to institution, it becomes difficult to assess their learning at a single point and then use that point to indicate what new learning might have occurred. By measuring student knowledge at senior year, it is difficult to know what parts of a transfer student's knowledge might be attributed to that institution. Since in most cases, assessment of student learning outcomes is measured across student populations, and often in aggregate, there is often no tracking of an individual student's movement through higher education.

Instituting a tracking system for assessing student learning across several institutions has been mentioned as a potential solution to this dilemma. Jeff Welsh (2002) used a nationwide sample to gather information about assessing transfer students. He identified several methods to do this. One of these best practices "in state-wide transfer student information systems is the ability to track student transfers among all post-secondary institutions within the state on a continuous basis" (p. 263). This is, however, difficult to do. Students often transfer from an institution in one state to one in another state, or from a private institution to a public one. Since there are no nationwide outcomes or standards for higher education, individual transfer students will transfer course credits from previous institutions, but there is no way currently for measuring the learning that a student might bring with her or him.

Technology

Changes in technology will change assessment. New computer technologies and software will have an impact on assessment. According to Marc Hall (2000), "Testing and assessment are prime candidates for technological innovation, as the pencil-and-paper, blue book, and fill-in-the-blank models of testing are nearing the end of their useful life. Just over the horizon are new methods, new mechanisms and new modes of test development, delivery, taking, and administration" (p. 15). Computerized scoring of student writing samples is already being used. For example, the Educational Testing Service uses an e-rater system to score writing samples electronically. Paperless large-scale tests are also available. Students can take the Collegiate Learning Assessment (CLA) completely online. The wide availability of the Internet has made access possible for many of these tests.

Computerized administration and scoring of tests offers several potential benefits. This type of system can save a great deal of time. Obviously if faculty are not spending time reading essays, they can focus more on teaching or research. And in many instances, students can get their test results quickly. Immediate feedback for students can be a strong motivator. Nevertheless, this type of system poses some potential problems. The system depends completely on access to appropriate technology. If a particular system goes down, the student might not be able to take the test or might not get the appropriate credit or score. There is a philosophical issue to this as well: Can a computer score written communication? In fact, by checking the inter-rater reliability between a human rater and a computerized rater, it is possible to track the correlation.

In addition to exams, technology can add to the storing and use of student learning data. Digital portfolios, Web folios, and e-portfolios are becoming common across many college campuses. Electronic portfolio systems allow students to keep specific work products that demonstrate learning outcomes in a single virtual space. Some institutions use these to follow student learning through their years at that institution; others use them for a single course. Elements of an e-portfolio might include specific assignments from a course, artifacts from a cocurricular activity, a journal or other types of reflection on learning, and digital images and videos reflecting other elements of student learning. These e-portfolio elements can be shared as appropriate from course to course, for overall institutional outcomes assessment, or even for students to demonstrate the skills they have learned to a potential employer.

Technology can also help to support the management of institutional-level assessment programs. By using an online management database, assessment directors can track program- or course-level assessment data. This provides a more formative approach to the assessment planning process since a director of assessment can view what a department has developed at any time. Because many of these assessment database management systems are Web based, institutions can use them to check alignment of institutional-, program-, and course-level outcomes and to share data across traditional disciplinary areas.

Technology will certainly provide a wider range of options for assessing student learning just as it has changed the way that teaching is often done. Maintaining vigilance, ensuring that assessment data that are gathered are valid and reliable, and making certain that data are shared appropriately can benefit the movement toward transformative assessment.

Increased Authentic Measures of Learning

Proponents of authentic assessment methods promote the value of using student performance on real-world tasks to measure student learning outcomes, rather than on the more traditional paper-and-pencil assessments (Sandoval & Wigle, 2006). The use of authentic assessment measures will increase as higher education develops methods for measuring learning outcomes in authentic ways. While basic knowledge and content can be assessed using multiple-choice or other objective measures, there is a growing call for measuring student learning that is richer and more subjective. This type of measure is more difficult to score because of the increased subjectivity and the potential breadth of the measure.

Recognition of the Complexity of Higher Education Outcomes

Learning is complex. Student learning at the postsecondary level should be multifaceted, complex, and difficult. Measuring this type of complex learning requires an assessment strategy that allows both qualitative and quantitative aspects while still remaining valid. "Any strategy that tries to enhance complex learning will be limited if it relies on formal learning. The reason is that formal learning may have its place but it is not authentic (in the sense that it is not the main shape that authentic learning takes) and it may be too de-contexted, even artificial, to be of much use in the workplace" (Knight & Banks, 2003, p. 49). Knight and Banks (2003) distinguish between formal learning, which may be complicated, such as memorizing formulas or facts, and informal learning, which involves critical thinking and the ability to apply knowledge to new situations or concepts.

Acknowledging that higher education should be identifying and trying to measure complex constructs and knowledge is important. But developing meaningful and appropriate measures that are not overly time-consuming is a difficult and ongoing task. Institutions that begin to look for assessment processes that are transformative will be more likely to explore areas of measuring complex and difficult-to-define concepts. Although there may never be a single perfect measure for learning outcomes focused on areas such as diversity, integrative learning, leadership, social justice, or global citizenship, it is certainly potentially possible to create a measure or even multiple measures of certain aspects of these constructs.

Intentional Alignment of the Educational Process

For some time, the assessment process has been focused on the mission and outcomes at the level of the department or program. Recent changes in accreditation standards have asked assessment plans to focus on the institutional level as well. *Constructive alignment*, a term first used by John Biggs (1999), refers to the alignment among stated student learning outcomes for a particular program and the specific assessment methods and grading criteria used for the course. The basic premise of the system is that the curriculum is designed so that learning activities and assessment tasks are aligned with the learning outcomes that are intended for the students to learn in the course. Biggs's constructive alignment concept is used specifically to align course-level learning outcomes with the assessment of student learning within the course.

This same principle can be applied to the transformative assessment process at the institutional level. The institutional mission should be aligned with the institutional-level outcomes, which should be aligned with the departmental and program outcomes, which should then be aligned with the individual course outcomes. Of course, there will be additions to the outcomes to ensure that they are discipline or program specific, and not all departments or programs will have all of the institutional-level outcomes represented in their listing of student learning outcomes. But there should be a basic sense of alignment throughout the process. Added to this, there must now be an alignment with the methods used to assess each of the outcomes. As John Biggs (1999, 2003) has pointed out, students' learning is constructed in part by the method used to measure learning. For example, students study differently for a multiple-choice exam than they do for an essay exam.

Writing a paper calls on different skills and results in a different type of learning than preparing for a debate. How student learning is measured will have an impact on how and how much they learn. Constructive alignment encourages faculty and institutions to be intentional about the design of the curriculum, and it can add transparency in understanding linkages between learning and assessment.

Assessing Collaboration and Teamwork

Collaboration and teamwork are consistently among the learning outcomes that employers ask for again and again (Association of American College and Universities, 2005). However, browsing through postsecondary mission statements reveals that few institutions place these items as a high priority. Leadership skills are often mentioned in mission statements, but team-based skills rarely are. However, looking deeper within an institution will show that often these are required skills at the course level. Many courses have a group project or some type of team-based learning activity. Michaelson, Knight, and Fink (2002) have created a teaching technique that allows students to become part of a team and learn teamwork skills as they learn specific course content. These types of collaborative and interpersonal skills are often not measured by departments or programs, but they often play a role in course content. And employers have indicated that they are looking for students who can work collaboratively. According to a recent survey of employers by the Association of American College and Universities (2007), 76 percent wanted colleges to place more emphasis on teamwork skills. Clearly this is a skill in demand.

The need for student skills in teamwork and other types of collaboration will increase in the years to come. The interest in designing and applying collaborative practices is continually growing in research and development, industry, education, and many other organizations. It stands to reason, then, that it is impossible for a single person or unit within an organization to have all the required information and skills to solve all of the increasingly complex problems that arise. Therefore, student skills in collaboration and teamwork are increasingly important to integrate knowledge, skills and abilities from a student's educational experience and into the workplace (Simonin, 1997).

Institutional incorporation of teamwork and collaborative skills will have to occur before these will begin to be measured across institutions. However, as calls from employers demonstrate the increasing need for these skills, institutions that want to keep their graduates competitive will begin to address these outcomes.

Strom and Strom (2002) suggest that several aspects of their collaborative-integration theory support the course-level assessment of student learning of teamwork skills:

- Students need to practice the teamwork skills that are required in the workplace.
- Perspective is enriched by incorporating learning sources from outside the school.
- Cultural and generational differences in viewpoints deserve student consideration.
- Assigning separate roles to team members increases the scope of group learning.
- Accountability can be determined by how well students perform particular roles.
- Observations about peer and self contributions to group work improve evaluation.
- Individual productivity can be motivated by anonymous recognition from peers [pp. 320–321].

As transformative assessment processes provide data to faculty, staff, and administrators, the need for reliable and valid measures of collaboration and teamwork will become more apparent. There is a significant amount of research on collaboration learning at the course level (for example, Cottel & Millis, 1994; Davidson & Worsham, 1992), and this information can be used to develop and implement powerful team and collaborative experiences for students that will benefit learning.

Team-Based Transformative Assessment

The concept of a team-based assessment model was developed by the Policy Center on the First Year of College (Swing, 2004). This process focuses on the need for the development of assessment practices within the institution that will benefit from the data. A team-based assessment model has these elements:

- Using local knowledge
- Honoring local expertise and professional knowledge
- Looking holistically at structures specific to the institution
- Creating appropriate professional and faculty development activities
- Developing a system that produces internal advocates for change
- An ongoing process that engages institutional members in debate, research, analysis, and improvement planning

A team-based assessment model incorporates the individual and often unique features of an institution. This could certainly create a university culture that appreciates and uses assessment of student learning outcomes to enhance overall institutional effectiveness. Since this model uses faculty and staff expertise and is an ongoing process, the institution will be able to observe the impact of assessment-based planning decisions and take the broader view of ongoing quality enhancement.

Conclusion

Transformative assessment is a meaningful and worthwhile process that will inform course, departmental, and campus-level decision making. This process must be appropriate, meaningful, sustainable, flexible, and ongoing, and it must use data for improvement with the potential for substantive change. Although the data collected can also be used to demonstrate outcomes to others for accountability purposes, transformative assessment is principally focused on how to strengthen student learning at the local level.

Carol Geary Schneider (2007) believes that assessment is an important, even necessary, tool as higher education moves forward. She has stated that "assessment is a crucial tool for helping colleges and universities set educational goals in the context of these social obligations; examine and report their own progress, and make needed improvements for their educational programs" (p. 3). She nevertheless expresses concern that current forms and measures for assessment are not used as a "positive resource" for faculty work and deeper learning for students. She advises, "There is only one useful way forward for assessment. And that is to adopt assessment practices that build from and reinforce the sources of higher education's historic strengths" (p. 3).

If the assessment process is going to make a difference in the future of higher education at more substantial levels than it has over the past three decades, the process must become more formative and encompass trust and dialogue. Higher education as a whole, and student learning in particular, is a complex, multifaceted concept. Oversimplifying the measurement process does a disservice to education, its current and future students, and all others who have a stake in the outcomes. Higher education must find a way to incorporate transformative assessment that is realistic and informative. Assessment for accountability will always be part of the overall assessment process, but it must not be the tail that wags the dog. Measuring student learning should always be, first and foremost, a formative process that is designed to enhance student learning at the local level.

Transformative assessment is about education with all of its richness and abounding potential. Much of what we know and how we learn will never be adequately and completely measured. But with the careful, inclusive, and intentional focus on transformation, the assessment process can lead us toward our vision of what higher education should be.

References

Allen, M. J. (2004). *Assessing academic programs in higher education.* Bolton, MA: Anker.

Alstete, J. (2004). *Accreditation matters: Achieving academic reorganization and renewal.* ASHE-ERIC Higher Education Report, Vol. 30(4). San Francisco: Jossey-Bass.

American Association of State Colleges and Universities. (2006). *Value-added assessment: Accountability's new frontier.* Washington, DC: Author.

The American Heritage Dictionary of the English Language, Fourth Edition. (2002). Appropriate. Boston: Houghton Mifflin. Retrieved June 8, 2007, from http://dictionary.reference.com/browse/appropriate.

Angelo, T. (1999). Doing assessment as if learning matters most. *AAHE Bulletin, 51*(9), 3–6.

Angelo, T., & Cross, P. (1993). *Classroom assessment techniques: A handbook for college teachers* (2nd ed.). San Francisco: Jossey-Bass.

Association of American College and Universities. (2005). *Liberal education outcomes: A preliminary report on student achievement in college.* Washington, DC: Author.

Association of American College and Universities. (2006). *Statement on Spellings Commission Report*. Retrieved August 4, 2007, from http://www.aacu.org/About/statements/Spellings9_26_06.cfmon.

Association of American Colleges and Universities. (2007). *College learning for the new global century*. Washington, DC: Author.

Astin, A. (1977). *Four critical years*. San Francisco: Jossey-Bass.

Banta, T. W. (2002). Characteristics of effective outcomes assessment: Foundations and examples. In T. W. Banta (Ed.), *Building a scholarship of assessment*. San Francisco: Jossey-Bass.

Banta, T. (2005). What draws campus leaders to embrace outcomes assessment? *Assessment Update, 17, 3*, 14–15.

Banta, T. (2007a). If we must compare . . . *Assessment Update, 19*(2), 3–4.

Banta, T. W. (2007b, Spring). Can assessment for accountability complement assessment for improvement? *Peer Review*, 9–12.

Banta, T. W., & Associates. (1993). *Making a difference: Outcomes of a decade of assessment in higher education*. San Francisco: Jossey-Bass.

Banta, T., & Kuh, G. (1998). A missing link in assessment. *Change, 30*, 40–47.

Bellas, M. L., & Toutkoushian, R. K. (1999). Faculty time allocations and research productivity: Gender, race, and family effects. *Review of Higher Education, 22*, 367–390.

Berberet, J. (1999). The professoriate and institutional citizenship. *Liberal Education, 85*, 32–40.

Bergquist, W. H., & Phillips, S. R. (1975). Components of an effective faculty development program. *Journal of Higher Education, 46*, 177–211.

Berheide, C. W. (2007). Doing less work, collecting better data: Using capstone courses to assess learning. *Peer Review, 9*, 27–30.

Biggs, J. (1999). *Teaching for quality learning at university: What the student does.* London: Society for Research into Higher Education and Open University Press.

Biggs, J. (2003). *Aligning teaching and assessment to curriculum objectives.* Lancaster, United Kingdom: Imaginative Curriculum Project, LTSN Generic Centre.

Biswas, R. R. (2006). *A supporting role: How accreditors can help promote the success of community college students.* Boston: Jobs for the Future.

Block, J. (1971). *Mastery learning: Theory and practice.* New York: Holt.

Bloom, B. (1968). Learning for mastery. *Evaluation Comment, 1*(2), 1–12.

Bok, D. C. (2006). *Our underachieving colleges: A candid look at how much students learn and why they should be learning more.* Princeton, NJ: Princeton University Press.

Boyer, E. (1990). *Scholarship reconsidered: Priorities of the professoriate.* Princeton, NJ: Carnegie Foundation for the Advancement of Teaching.

Brown, K. (2001). Community college strategies: Why aren't faculty jumping on the assessment bandwagon and what can be done to encourage their involvement? *Assessment Update, 13,* 8–10.

Carey, K. (2007, September/October). Truth without action: The myth of higher-education accountability. *Change,* 24–29.

Centra, J. A. (1976). *Faculty development practices in US colleges and universities.* Princeton, NJ: Educational Testing Service.

Chickering, A. W. (1969). *Education and identity.* San Francisco: Jossey-Bass.

Cottell, P. G., Jr., & Millis, B. J. (1994). Complex cooperative learning structures for college and university courses. *To Improve the Academy: Resources for Faculty, Instructional, and Organizational Development, 13,* 285–307.

Cottrell, S. A., & Jones, E. A. (2002). A snapshot of scholarship of teaching and learning initiatives: Using assessment results to improve student learning and development. *Assessment Update, 14,* 6–7.

Council for Higher Education Accreditation. (2006). *Talking points: Commission on the Future of Higher Education, regional hearings and accreditation.* Retrieved August 3, 2007, from http://www.chea.org/Government/Talking-Points.pdf.

Council for the Advancement of Standards in Higher Education. (2007). *Frameworks for addressing learning and development outcomes.* Retrieved November 1, 2007, from http://www.cas.edu/.

Cumberland County College. Office of Institutional Research. (2005). Assessment: Advancing student learning. In *Office for Institutional Research Newsletter, 4.* Vineland, NJ: Author. Retrieved February 11, 2008, from http://www.cccnj.edu/facultyStaff/planningResearch/oir/oir_studies/newsletters/newsletterDecember2005.pdf.

Cutler, W. W. (2006). The scholarship of teaching and learning and student assessment. *History Teacher, 40,* 69–74.

Davenport, C. A. (2001). How frequently should accreditation standards change? In J. L. Ratcliff, E. S. Lubinescu, & M. A. Gaffney (Eds.), *How accreditation influences assessment* (pp. 67–82). San Francisco: Jossey-Bass.

Davidson, N., & Worsham, T. (Eds.). (1992). *Enhancing thinking through cooperative learning.* New York: Teachers College Press.

Dodd, A. H. (2004). Accreditation as a catalyst for institutional effectiveness. *New Directions for Institutional Research, 123,* 13–25.

Dooris, M. J. (1998). Strategies to involve faculty in assessment: Penn State. *Assessment Update, 10,* 5, 12.

Eaton, J. (2007, September/October). Institutions, accreditors, and the federal government: Redefining their "appropriate relationship." *Change,* 16–23.

Ehrenberg, R. G. (2005, Fall). Method or madness? Inside the *U.S. News and World Report* college rankings. *Journal of College Admission,* 29–35.

Ewell, P. (1999). Assessment of higher education quality: Promise and politics. In S. J. Messick (Ed.), *Assessment in higher education: Issues of access, quality, student development and public policy* (pp. 147–156). Mahwah, NJ: Erlbaum.

Ewell, P. (2002a). An emerging scholarship: A brief history of assessment.
In T. Banta & Associates (Eds.), *Building a scholarship of assessment.*
San Francisco: Jossey-Bass.

Ewell, P. (2002b). *Perpetual movement: Assessment after twenty years.* Boulder, CO:
National Center for Higher Education Management Systems. Retrieved August 23,
2007, from http://www.teaglefoundation.org/learning/pdf/2002_ewell.pdf.

Faculty Survey of Student Engagement. (2006). *Faculty time.* Retrieved
September 5, 2007, from http://fsse.iub.edu/html/FSSE_2006_Faculty_Time.cfm.

Farmer, D. W. (1999). Course-embedded assessment: A catalyst for realizing the
paradigm shift from teaching to learning. *Journal of Staff, Program and Organizational Development, 16,* 199–211.

Fendrich, L. (2007, June 8). A pedagogical straitjacket. *Chronicle of Higher
Education,* B6.

Finkelstein, M. J. (1984). *The American academic profession: A synthesis of social
scientific inquiry since World War II.* Columbus: Ohio State University.

Gaff, J. G. (1975). *Toward faculty renewal.* San Francisco: Jossey-Bass.

Gerretson, H., & Golson, E. (2005). Synopsis of the use of course-embedded
assessment in a medium sized public university's general education program.
Journal of General Education, 54, 139–149.

Glassick, C. E., Huber, M. T., and Maeroff, G. I. (1997). *Scholarship assessed:
Evaluation of the professoriate.* San Francisco: Jossey-Bass.

Graham, A., & Thompson, N. (2001). Broken ranks. *Washington Monthly.*
Retrieved August 18, 2007, from www.washingtonmonthly.com/features/2001/
0109.graham.thompson.html.

Griffith, S. R., Day, S. B., Scott, J. E., & Smallwood, R. A. (1996, May). *First
year report: Progress made on a plan to integrate planning, budgeting, assessment,
and quality principles to achieve institutional improvement.* Paper presented at
the 36th Annual Forum of the Association for Institutional Research,
Albuquerque, NM.

Hall, M. E. (2000). A streamlined future for assessment. *Thrust for Educational Leadership, 29*, 15.

Higher Learning Commission/NCA. (2003). *Assessment of student academic achievement: Assessment culture matrix.* Chicago: Higher Learning Commission/NCA. Retrieved November 30, 2006, from http://www.ncahlc.org/download/97ASSESS.pdf.

Huba, M., & Freed, J. E. (2000). *Learner-centered assessment on college campuses: Shifting the focus from teaching to learning.* Needham Heights, MA: Allyn & Bacon.

Hutchings, P. (1996, November–December). Building a new culture of teaching and learning. *About Campus,* 4–8.

Hutchings, P., & Marchese, T. (1990). Watching assessment: Questions, stories, prospects. *Change, 22,* 12–38.

Jacobs, J. A. (2004). The faculty time divide. *Sociological Forum, 19,* 3–27.

Jorgensen, M. (2007, November). *Accreditation: Don't worry, be happy.* Presentation at the 2007 Assessment Institute, Indianapolis, IN.

Knight, P. T., & Banks, W. M. (2003). The assessment of complex learning outcomes. *Global Journal of Engineering Education, 7,* 39–50.

Kramer, P. I. (2006). Assessment and the fear of punishment: How the protection of anonymity positively influenced the design and outcomes of postsecondary assessment. *Assessment and Evaluation in Higher Education, 31,* 597–609.

Kuh, G. (1996). Guiding principles for creating seamless learning environments for undergraduates. *Journal of College Student Development, 37,* 135–148.

Kuh, G., & Banta, T. (2000, January/February). Faculty-student affairs collaboration on assessment: Lessons from the field, *About Campus,* 4–11.

Lederman, D. (2007). *When is student learning "good enough"?* Retrieved November 1, 2007, from http://insidehighered.com/news/2007/02/23/accredit.

Light, R. J. (2001). *Making the most of college: Students speak their minds.* Cambridge, MA: Harvard University Press.

Lopez, C. (2002). Assessment of student learning: Challenges and strategies. *Journal of Academic Librarianship, 28*(6), 356–367.

Madison, B. (2001). *Assessment: The burden of a name.* Washington, DC: Math Association of America. Retrieved August 23, 2007, from http://www.maa.org/saum/articles/AssessmentTheBurdenofaName.html.

Magolda, P. M. (2005). Proceed with caution: Uncommon wisdom about academic and student affairs partnerships. *About Campus, 9,* 16–21.

Michaelson, L. K., Knight, A. B., & Fink, L. D. (2002). *Team based learning: A transformative use of small groups in college teaching.* Sterling, VA: Stylus.

Middle States Commission on Higher Education. (2005). *Assessing student learning and institutional effectiveness: Understanding Middle States' expectations.* Philadelphia: Author.

Moloney, J., & Tello, S. (2003). Achieving quality and scale in online education through transformative assessment: A case study. In J. Bourne & J. Moore (Eds.), *Elements of quality in online education, Volume 5.* Needham, MA: Sloan-C and the Sloan Center for Online Education.

Mueller, J. (2006). *Authentic assessment toolkit.* Retrieved October 25, 2007, from http://jonathan.mueller.faculty.noctrl.edu/toolbox/whatisit.htm.

Musil, C. M. (1992). *Students at the center: Feminist assessment.* Washington, DC: Association of American Colleges and National Women's Studies Association.

National Research Council. (2001). *Knowing what students know: The science and design of educational assessment.* Washington, DC: National Academy Press.

Neumann, A., & Terosky, A. (2003). *Toward images of reciprocity in faculty service: Insights from a study of the early post-tenure career.* Unpublished manuscript.

Nichols, J. O. (1995). *A practitioner's handbook for institutional effectiveness and student learning outcomes assessment implementation.* New York: Agathon.

Ohmann, R. (2000). Historical reflections on accountability. *Academe, 86,* 24–29.

Palomba, C. A., & Banta, T. W. (1999). *Assessment essentials*. San Francisco: Jossey-Bass.

Pascarella, E., & Terenzini, P. (1991). *How college affects students: Findings and insights from twenty years of research*. San Francisco: Jossey-Bass.

Perry, W. G. (1999). *Forms of ethical and intellectual development in the college years*. San Francisco: Jossey-Bass.

Peterson, M. W., & Vaughan, D. (2002). Promoting academic improvement: Organizational and administrative dynamics that support student assessment. In T. Banta & Associates (Eds.), *Building a scholarship of assessment* (pp. 26–46). San Francisco: Jossey-Bass.

Peterson's. (2008). *Peterson's Four Year Colleges 2008*. Lawrenceville, NJ: Author.

Pew Higher Education Research Group. (1996). Shared purposes. *Policy Perspectives, 6*, 1–8.

Popham, J. W. (2006, February). Assessment for learning: An endangered species? *Educational Leadership*, 82–83.

Ratcliff, J. L., Lubinescu, E. S., & Gaffney, M. A. (2001). *How accreditation influences assessment*. San Francisco: Jossey-Bass.

Rogers, J. T. (1997). Assessment in accreditation: Has it made a difference? *Assessment Update, 9*, 1–2, 15.

Sandovol, P. A., & Wigle, S. E. (2006). Building a unit assessment system: Creating a quality evaluation of candidate performance. *Education, 126*, 640–652.

Schilling, K. (2006). Assessment methods should match institutional goals. *Academic Leader, 22*, 2, 6.

Schneider, C. G. (2007). The way forward for assessment. *Liberal Education, 93*, 2–3.

Schroeder, C. C. (1999). Forging educational partnerships that advance student learning. In G. S. Bliming, E. Whitt, & Associates (Eds.), *Good practice in student affairs: Principles to foster student learning* (pp. 133–156). San Francisco: Jossey-Bass.

Schuh, J. H., Upcraft, M. L., & Associates. (2001). *Assessment practice in student affairs: An applications manual.* San Francisco: Jossey-Bass.

Shavelson, R. (2007a). *A brief history of student learning assessment: How we got where we are and a proposal for where to go next.* Washington, DC: Association of American Colleges and Universities.

Shavelson, R. (2007b). Assessing student learning responsibly: From history to an audacious proposal. *Change, 39,* 26–33.

Shulman, L. (2007). Counting and recounting: Assessment and the quest for accountability. *Change, 39,* 20–25.

Simonin, B. L. (1997). The importance of collaborative know-how: An empirical test of the learning organization. *Academy of Management Journal, 40,* 1150–1174.

Sloane, K., Wilson, M., & Samson, S. (1996). *Designing an embedded assessment system: From principles to practice.* Berkeley: University of California.

Smith, K. K. (2005). From coexistence to collaboration: A call for partnership between academic and student affairs. *Journal of Cognitive Affective Learning, 2,* 16–20.

Southern Association of Colleges and Schools, Commission on Colleges. (2006). *Integrity and accuracy in institutional representation: Policy statement.* Retrieved February 10, 2008, from http://www.sacscoc.org/pdf/081705/integrity.pdf.

Southern Illinois University–Edwardsville. (2008). *Classroom assessment techniques.* Retrieved February 11, 2008, from http://www.siue.edu/~deder/assess/catmain.html.

St. Ours, P. A., & Corsello, M. (1998). Faculty driven assessment: A collaborative model that works. *Assessment Update, 10,* 6.

Strom, P. S., & Strom, R. D. (2002). Overcoming limitations of cooperative learning among community college students. *Community College Journal of Research and Practice, 26,* 315–331.

Sullivan, M. M., & Wilds, P. C. (2001). Institutional effectiveness: More than measure objectives, more than student assessment. *Assessment Update, 13,* 4–5, 13.

Swing, R. L. (Ed.). (2004). *Proving and improving, Vol. 2: Tools and techniques for assessing the first college year* (Monograph No. 37). Columbia: University of South Carolina, National Resource Center for the First-Year Experience and Students in Transition.

Tinto, V. (1975). Dropout from higher education: A theoretical synthesis of recent research. *Review of Educational Research, 45*, 89–127.

U.S. Department of Education. (2006a). *A test of leadership: Charting the future of U.S. higher education*. Washington, DC: Author.

U.S. Department of Education. (2006b). *Secretary Spellings' prepared remarks at the National Press Club: An action plan for higher education*. Retrieved February 10, 2008, from http://www.ed.gov/news/speeches/2006/09/09262006.html.

University of Central Florida. (2004). *Program assessment handbook*. Orlando, FL: Author.

Upcraft, M. L., & Schuh, J. H. (1996). *Assessment in student affairs: A guide for practitioners*. San Francisco: Jossey-Bass.

Walvoord, B. E. (2004). *Assessment clear and simple*. San Francisco: Jossey-Bass.

Ward, K. (2003). *Internal service: Faculty at work as institutional and disciplinary citizens*. ASHE-ERIC Higher Education Report, Vol. 29(5). San Francisco: Jossey-Bass.

Washington State University. (2003). *Assessing transformation: Quick reference*. Retrieved August 28, 2007, from http://www.educause.edu/ir/library/pdf/EDU0251.pdf.

Wehlburg, C. (1999). How to get the ball rolling: Beginning an assessment program on your campus. *AAHE Bulletin, 51*, 7–9.

Wehlburg, C. (2002). More than a thermometer: Using assessment effectively. In G. Wheeler (Ed.), *Teaching and learning in college: A resource for educators* (4th ed., pp. 177–199). Lorain, OH: Info-Tec.

Wehlburg, C. (2004). Using data to enhance college teaching: Course and departmental assessment results as a faculty development tool. In S. Chadwick & D. Robertson (Eds.), *To improve the academy: Resources for faculty, instructional, and organizational development, Vol. 23*. Bolton, MA: Anker.

Wehlburg, C. (2006). *Meaningful course revision: Enhancing academic engagement using student learning data*. Bolton, MA: Anker.

Wehlburg, C. (2007). Closing the feedback loop is not enough: The assessment spiral. *Assessment Update, 19*(2), 1–2, 15.

Welsh, J. F. (2002). Assessing the transfer function: Benchmarking best practices from state higher education agencies. *Assessment and Evaluation in Higher Education, 27*, 257–258.

Welsh, J. F., & Metcalf, J. (2003a). Faculty and administrative support for institutional effectiveness activities: A bridge across the chasm? *Journal of Higher Education, 74*, 445–468.

Welsh, J. F., & Metcalf, J. (2003b). Cultivating faculty support for institutional effectiveness activities: Benchmarking best practices. *Assessment and Evaluation in Higher Education, 28*, 33–45.

Wiggins, G. P. (1993). *Assessing student performance*. San Francisco: Jossey-Bass.

Wilson, M., & Sloane, K. (2000). From principles to practice: An embedded assessment system. *Applied Measurement in Education, 13*, 181–208.

Wolf, R., & Harris, O. (1994). Using assessment to develop a culture of evidence. In D. Halpern & Associates (Eds.), *Changing college classrooms: New teaching and learning strategies for an increasingly complex world* (pp. 271–278). San Francisco: Jossey-Bass.

Wright, B. D. (2005). The way to a faculty member's head is through the discipline. *Assessment Update, 17*, 1–2, 12–13.

Yale Daily News Staff. (2008). *Insider's guide to colleges—2008*. New York: St. Martin's Press.

Young, K. E., Chambers, C. M., & Kells, H. R. (1983). *Understanding accreditation.* San Francisco: Jossey-Bass.

Zeller, W., Hinni, J., & Eison, J. (1989). Creating educational partnerships between academic and student affairs. In D. C. Roberts (Ed.), *Designing campus activities to foster a sense of community* (pp. 49–59). New Directions for Student Services, no. 48. San Francisco: Jossey-Bass.

Index

Note to Index: An e following a page number denotes an exhibit on that page; an f following a page number denotes a figure on that page; a t following a page number denotes a table on that page.